FAST LADIES

FEMALE RACING DRIVERS

1888-1970

VELOCE PUBLISHING
THE PUBLISHER OF FINE AUTOMOTIVE BOOKS

Also from Veloce Publishing:

Speedpro Series

4-cylinder Engine – How To Blueprint & Build A Short Block For High Performance (Hammill)
Alfa Romeo DOHC High-performance Manual (Kartalamakis)
Alfa Romeo V6 Engine High-performance Manual (Kartalamakis)
BMC 998cc A-series Engine – How To Power Tune (Hammill)
1275cc A-series High-performance Manual (Hammill)
Camshafts – How To Choose & Time Them For Maximum Power (Hammill)
Competition Car Datalogging Manual, The (Templeman)
Cylinder Heads – How To Build, Modify & Power Tune Updated & Revised Edition (Burgess & Gollan)
Distributor-type Ignition Systems – How To Build & Power Tune New 3rd Edition (Hammill)
Fast Road Car – How To Plan And Build Revised & Updated Colour New Edition (Stapleton)
Ford SOHC 'Pinto' & Sierra Cosworth DOHC Engines – How To Power Tune Updated & Enlarged Edition (Hammill)
Ford V8 – How To Power Tune Small Block Engines (Hammill)
Harley-Davidson Evolution Engines – How To Build & Power Tune (Hammill)
Holley Carburetors – How To Build & Power Tune Revised & Updated Edition (Hammill)
Honda Civic Type R, High-Performance Manual (Cowland & Clifford)
Jaguar XK Engines – How To Power Tune Revised & Updated Colour Edition (Hammill)
MG Midget & Austin-Healey Sprite – How To Power Tune New 3rd Edition (Stapleton)
MGB 4-cylinder Engine – How To Power Tune (Burgess)
MGB V8 Power – How To Give Your, Third Colour Edition (Williams)
MGB, MGC & MGB V8 – How To Improve New 2nd Edition (Williams)
Mini Engines – How To Power Tune On A Small Budget Colour Edition (Hammill)
Motorcycle-engined Racing Car – How To Build (Pashley)
Motorsport – Getting Started in (Collins)
Nissan GT-R High-performance Manual, The (Gorodji)
Nitrous Oxide High-performance Manual, The (Langfield)
Rover V8 Engines – How To Power Tune (Hammill)
Sportscar & Kitcar Suspension & Brakes – How To Build & Modify Revised 3rd Edition (Hammill)
SU Carburettor High-performance Manual (Hammill)
Successful Low-Cost Rally Car, How to Build a (Young)
Suzuki 4x4 – How To Modify For Serious Off-road Action (Richardson)
Tiger Avon Sportscar – How To Build Your Own Updated & Revised 2nd Edition (Dudley)
TR2, 3 & TR4 – How To Improve (Williams)
TR5, 250 & TR6 – How To Improve (Williams)
TR7 & TR8 – How To Improve (Williams)
V8 Engine – How To Build A Short Block For High Performance (Hammill)
Volkswagen Beetle Suspension, Brakes & Chassis – How To Modify For High Performance (Hale)
Volkswagen Bus Suspension, Brakes & Chassis – How To Modify For High Performance (Hale)
Weber DCOE, & Dellorto DHLA Carburetors – How To Build & Power Tune 3rd Edition (Hammill)

Those Were The Days ... Series

Alpine Trials & Rallies 1910-1973 (Pfundner)
American Trucks of the 1950s (Mort)
Anglo-American Cars From the 1930s to the 1970s (Mort)
Austerity Motoring (Bobbitt)
Austins, The last real (Peck)
Brighton National Speed Trials (Gardiner)
British Lorries Of The 1950s (Bobbitt)
British Lorries of the 1960s (Bobbitt)
British Touring Car Championship, The (Collins)
British Police Cars (Walker)
British Woodies (Peck)
Café Racer Phenomenon, The (Walker)
Dune Buggy Phenomenon (Hale)
Dune Buggy Phenomenon Volume 2 (Hale)
Hot Rod & Stock Car Racing in Britain In The 1980s (Neil)
Last Real Austins, The, 1946-1959 (Peck)
MG's Abingdon Factory (Moylan)
Motor Racing At Brands Hatch In The Seventies (Parker)
Motor Racing At Brands Hatch In The Eighties (Parker)
Motor Racing At Crystal Palace (Collins)
Motor Racing At Goodwood In The Sixties (Gardiner)
Motor Racing At Nassau In The 1950s & 1960s (O'Neil)
Motor Racing At Oulton Park In The 1960s (McFadyen)
Motor Racing At Oulton Park In The 1970s (McFadyen)
Superprix - The Story of Birmingham's Motor Race (Collins & Page)
Three Wheelers (Bobbitt)

Enthusiast's Restoration Manual Series

Citroën 2CV, How To Restore (Porter)
Classic Car Bodywork, How To Restore (Thaddeus)
Classic British Car Electrical Systems (Astley)
Classic Car Electrics (Thaddeus)
Classic Cars, How To Paint (Thaddeus)
Reliant Regal, How To Restore (Payne)
Triumph TR2, 3, 3A, 4 & 4A, How To Restore (Williams)
Triumph TR5/250 & 6, How To Restore (Williams)
Triumph TR7/8, How To Restore (Williams)
Volkswagen Beetle, How To Restore (Tyler)
VW Bay Window Bus (Paxton)
Yamaha FS1-E, How To Restore (Watts)

Essential Buyer's Guide Series

Alfa GT (Booker)
Alfa Romeo Spider Giulia (Booker & Talbott)
BMW GS (Henshaw)
BSA Bantam (Henshaw)
BSA Twins (Henshaw)
Citroën 2CV (Paxton)
Citroën ID & DS (Heilig)
Fiat 500 & 600 (Bobbitt)
Ford Capri (Paxton)
Jaguar E-type 3.8 & 4.2-litre (Crespin)
Jaguar E-type V12 5.3-litre (Crespin)
Jaguar XJ 1995-2003 (Crespin)
Jaguar/Daimler XJ6, XJ12 & Sovereign (Crespin)
Jaguar/Daimler XJ40 (Crespin)
Jaguar XJ-S (Crespin)
MGB & MGB GT (Williams)
Mercedes-Benz 280SL-560DSL Roadsters (Bass)
Mercedes-Benz 'Pagoda' 230SL, 250SL & 280SL Roadsters & Coupés (Bass)
Mini (Paxton)
Morris Minor & 1000 (Newell)
Porsche 928 (Hemmings)
Rolls-Royce Silver Shadow & Bentley T-Series (Bobbitt)
Subaru Impreza (Hobbs)
Triumph Bonneville (Henshaw)
Triumph Stag (Mort & Fox)
Triumph TR6 (Williams)
VW Beetle (Cservenka & Copping)
VW Bus (Cservenka & Copping)
VW Golf GTI (Cservenka & Copping)

Auto-Graphics Series

Fiat-based Abarths (Sparrow)
Jaguar MkI & II Saloons (Sparrow)
Lambretta Li Series Scooters (Sparrow)

Rally Giants Series

Audi Quattro (Robson)
Austin Healey 100-6 & 3000 (Robson)
Fiat 131 Abarth (Robson)
Ford Escort MkI (Robson)
Ford Escort RS Cosworth & World Rally Car (Robson)
Ford Escort RS1800 (Robson)
Lancia Stratos (Robson)
Mini Cooper/Mini Cooper S (Robson)
Peugeot 205 T16 (Robson)
Subaru Impreza (Robson)
Toyota Celica GT4 (Robson)

WSC Giants

Ferrari 312P & 312PB (Collins & McDonough)

Battle Cry! Original Military Uniforms of the World
Soviet General & field rank officers uniforms: 1955 to 1991 (Streather)

General

1½-litre GP Racing 1961-1965 (Whitelock)
AC Two-litre Saloons & Buckland Sportscars (Archibald)
Alfa Romeo Giulia Coupé GT & GTA (Tipler)
Alfa Romeo Montreal – The dream car that came true (Taylor)
Alfa Romeo Montreal – The Essential Companion (Taylor)
Alfa Tipo 33 (McDonough & Collins)
Alpine & Renault – The Development Of The Revolutionary Turbo F1 Car 1968 to 1979 (Smith)
Anatomy Of The Works Minis (Moylan)
André Lefebvre, and the cars he created at Voisin and Citroën (Beck)
Armstrong-Siddeley (Smith)
Autodrome (Collins & Ireland)
Automotive A-Z, Lane's Dictionary Of Automotive Terms (Lane)
Automotive Mascots (Kay & Springate)
Bahamas Speed Weeks, The (O'Neil)
Bentley Continental, Corniche And Azure (Bennett)
Bentley MkVI, Rolls-Royce Silver Wraith, Dawn & Cloud/Bentley R & S-Series (Nutland)
BMC Competitions Department Secrets (Turner, Chambers Browning)
BMW 5-Series (Cranswick)
BMW Z-Cars (Taylor)
BMW Boxer Twins 1970-1995 Bible, The (Falloon)
Britains Farm Model Balers & Combines 1967 to 2007 (Pullen)
British 250cc Racing Motorcycles (Pereira)
British Cars, The Complete Catalogue Of, 1895-1975 (Culshaw & Horrobin)
BRM – A Mechanic's Tale (Salmon)
BRM V16 (Ludvigsen)
BSA Bantam Bible, The (Henshaw)
Bugatti Type 40 (Price)
Bugatti 46/50 Updated Edition (Price & Arbey)
Bugatti T44 & T49 (Price & Arbey)
Bugatti 57 2nd Edition (Price)
Caravans, The Illustrated History 1919-1959 (Jenkinson)
Caravans, The Illustrated History From 1960 (Jenkinson)
Carrera Panamericana, La (Tipler)
Chrysler 300 – America's Most Powerful Car 2nd Edition (Ackerson)
Chrysler PT Cruiser (Ackerson)
Citroën DS (Bobbitt)
Classic British Car Electrical Systems (Astley)
Cliff Allison – From The Fells To Ferrari (Gauld)
Cobra – The Real Thing! (Legate)
Concept Cars, How to illustrate and design (Dewey)
Cortina – Ford's Bestseller (Robson)
Coventry Climax Racing Engines (Hammill)
Daimler SP250 New Edition (Long)
Datsun Fairlady Roadster To 280ZX – The Z-Car Story (Long)
Diecast Toy Cars of the 1950s & 1960s (Ralston)
Dino – The V6 Ferrari (Long)
Dodge Challenger & Plymouth Barracuda (Grist)
Dodge Charger – Enduring Thunder (Ackerson)
Dodge Dynamite! (Grist)
Donington (Boddy)
Draw & Paint Cars – How To (Gardiner)
Drive On The Wild Side, A – 20 Extreme Driving Adventures From Around The World (Weaver)
Ducati 750 Bible, The (Falloon)
Ducati 860, 900 And Mille Bible, The (Falloon)
Dune Buggy, Building A – The Essential Manual (Shakespeare)
Dune Buggy Files (Hale)
Dune Buggy Handbook (Hale)
Edward Turner: The Man Behind The Motorcycles (Clew)
Fiat & Abarth 124 Spider & Coupé (Tipler)
Fiat & Abarth 500 & 600 2nd Edition (Bobbitt)
Fiats, Great Small (Ward)
Fine Art Of The Motorcycle Engine, The (Peirce)
Ford F100/F150 Pick-up 1948-1996 (Ackerson)
Ford F150 Pick-up 1997-2005 (Ackerson)
Ford GT – Then, And Now (Streather)
Ford GT40 (Legate)
Ford In Miniature (Olson)
Ford Model Y (Roberts)
Ford Thunderbird From 1954, The Book Of The (Long)
Formula 5000 Motor Racing, Back then ... and back now (Lawson)
Forza Minardi! (Vigar)
Funky Mopeds (Skelton)
Gentleman Jack (Gauld)
GM In Miniature (Olson)
GT – The World's Best GT Cars 1953-73 (Dawson)
Hillclimbing & Sprinting – The Essential Manual (Short & Wilkinson)
Honda NSX (Long)
Intermeccanica - The Story of the Prancing Bull (McCredie & Reisner)
Jaguar, The Rise Of (Price)
Jaguar XJ-S (Long)
Jeep CJ (Ackerson)
Jeep Wrangler (Ackerson)
John Chatham - 'Mr Big Healey' – The Official Biography (Burr)
Karmann-Ghia Coupé & Convertible (Bobbitt)
Lamborghini Miura Bible, The (Sackey)
Lambretta Bible, The (Davies)
Lancia 037 (Collins)
Lancia Delta HF Integrale (Blaettel & Wagner)
Land Rover, The Half-ton Military (Cook)
Laverda Twins & Triples Bible 1968-1986 (Falloon)
Lea-Francis Story, The (Price)
Lexus Story, The (Long)
little book of smart, the New Edition (Jackson)
Lola – The Illustrated History (1957-1977) (Starkey)
Lola – All The Sports Racing & Single-seater Racing Cars 1978-1997 (Starkey)
Lola T70 – The Racing History & Individual Chassis Record 4th Edition (Starkey)
Lotus 49 (Oliver)
Marketingmobiles, The Wonderful Wacky World Of (Hale)
Mazda MX-5/Miata 1.6 Enthusiast's Workshop Manual (Grainger & Shoemark)
Mazda MX-5/Miata 1.8 Enthusiast's Workshop Manual (Grainger & Shoemark)
Mazda MX-5 Miata: The Book Of The World's Favourite Sportscar (Long)
Mazda MX-5 Miata Roadster (Long)
Maximum Mini (Booij)
MGA (Price Williams)
MGB & MGB GT– Expert Guide (Auto-doc Series) (Williams)
MGB Electrical Systems Updated & Revised Edition (Astley)
Micro Caravans (Jenkinson)
Micro Trucks (Mort)
Microcars At Large! (Quellin)
Mini Cooper – The Real Thing! (Tipler)
Mitsubishi Lancer Evo, The Road Car & WRC Story (Long)
Montlhéry, The Story Of The Paris Autodrome (Boddy)
Morgan Maverick (Lawrence)
Morris Minor, 60 Years On The Road (Newell)
Moto Guzzi Sport & Le Mans Bible, The (Falloon)
Motor Movies – The Posters! (Veysey)
Motor Racing – Reflections Of A Lost Era (Carter)
Motorcycle Apprentice (Cakebread)
Motorcycle Road & Racing Chassis Designs (Noakes)
Motorhomes, The Illustrated History (Jenkinson)
Motorsport In colour, 1950s (Wainwright)
Nissan 300ZX & 350Z – The Z-Car Story (Long)
Nissan GT-R Supercar: Born to race (Gorodji)
Off-Road Giants! – Heroes of 1960s Motorcycle Sport (Westlake)
Pass The Theory And Practical Driving Tests (Gibson & Hoole)
Peking To Paris 2007 (Young)
Plastic Toy Cars Of The 1950s & 1960s (Ralston)
Pocket Guide to Britains Farm Model & Toy Tractors 1998-2008 (Pullen)
Pontiac Firebird (Cranswick)
Porsche Boxster (Long)
Porsche 356 (2nd Edition) (Long)
Porsche 908 (Födisch, Neßhöver, Roßbach, Schwarz & Roßbach)
Porsche 911 Carrera – The Last Of The Evolution (Corlett)
Porsche 911R, RS & RSR, 4th Edition (Starkey)
Porsche 911 – The Definitive History 1963-1971 (Long)
Porsche 911 – The Definitive History 1971-1977 (Long)
Porsche 911 – The Definitive History 1977-1987 (Long)
Porsche 911 – The Definitive History 1987-1997 (Long)
Porsche 911 – The Definitive History 1997-2004 (Long)
Porsche 911SC 'Super Carrera' – The Essential Companion (Streather)
Porsche 914 & 914-6: The Definitive History Of The Road & Competition Cars (Long)
Porsche 924 (Long)
Porsche 928 (Long)
Porsche 944 (Long)
Porsche 964, 993 & 996 Data Plate Code Breaker (Streather)
Porsche 993 'King Of Porsche' – The Essential Companion (Streather)
Porsche 996 'Supreme Porsche' – The Essential Companion (Streather)
Porsche Racing Cars – 1953 To 1975 (Long)
Porsche Racing Cars – 1976 To 2005 (Long)
Porsche – The Rally Story (Meredith)
Porsche: Three Generations Of Genius (Meredith)
RAC Rally Action! (Gardiner)
Rallye Sport Fords: The Inside Story (Moreton)
Redman, Jim – 6 Times World Motorcycle Champion: The Autobiography (Redman)
Rolls-Royce Silver Shadow/Bentley T Series Corniche & Camargue Revised & Enlarged Edition (Bobbitt)
Rolls-Royce Silver Spirit, Silver Spur & Bentley Mulsanne 2nd Edition (Bobbitt)
Russian Motor Vehicles (Kelly)
RX-7 – Mazda's Rotary Engine Sportscar (Updated & Revised New Edition) (Long)
Save the Triumph Bonneville! - The inside story of the Meriden workers' co-op (Rosamond)
Scooters & Microcars, The A-Z Of Popular (Dan)
Scooter Lifestyle (Grainger)
Singer Story: Cars, Commercial Vehicles, Bicycles & Motorcycle (Atkinson)
SM – Citroën's Maserati-engined Supercar (Long & Claverol)
Speedway - Auto Racing's Ghost Tracks (Collins & Ireland)
Subaru Impreza: The Road Car And WRC Story (Long)
Supercar, How To Build your own (Thompson)
Tales from the Toolbox (Oliver)
Taxi! The Story Of The 'London' Taxicab (Bobbitt)
Tinplate Toy Cars Of The 1950s & 1960s (Ralston)
Toleman Story, The (Hilton)
Toyota Celica & Supra, The Book Of Toyota's Sports Coupés (Long)
Toyota MR2 Coupés & Spyders (Long)
Triumph Motorcycles & The Meriden Factory (Hancox)
Triumph Speed Twin & Thunderbird Bible (Woolridge)
Triumph Tiger Cub Bible (Estall)
Triumph Trophy Bible (Woolridge)
Triumph TR6 (Kimberley)
Unraced (Collins)
Velocette Motorcycles – MSS To Thruxton Updated & Revised (Burris)
Virgil Exner – Visioneer: The Official Biography Of Virgil M Exner Designer Extraordinaire (Grist)
Volkswagen Bus Book, The (Bobbitt)
Volkswagen Bus Or Van To Camper, How To Convert (Porter)
Volkswagens Of The World (Glen)
VW Beetle Cabriolet (Bobbitt)
VW Beetle – The Car Of The 20th Century (Copping)
VW Bus – 40 Years Of Splitties, Bays & Wedges (Copping)
VW Bus Book, The (Bobbitt)
VW Golf: Five Generations Of Fun (Copping & Cservenka)
VW – The Air-cooled Era (Copping)
VW T5 Camper Conversion Manual (Porter)
VW Campers (Copping)
Works Minis, The Last (Purves & Brenchley)
Works Rally Mechanic (Moylan)

From Veloce Publishing's new imprint: Hubble & Hattie

Winston, The dog who loved me (Hilmar Klute)

www.veloce.co.uk

Published in April 2009 by Veloce Publishing Limited, 33 Trinity Street, Dorchester DT1 1TT, England. Fax 01305 268864/e-mail info@veloce.co.uk/web www.veloce.co.uk or www.velocebooks.com.
ISBN: 978-1-84584-225-3 /UPC: 636847042257
Originally published by ETAI in 2007. All copy translated from the original French edition by Studyhood: www.studyhood.com/e-mail support@studyhood.com

© Jean-François Bouzanquet and Veloce Publishing 2009. All rights reserved. With the exception of quoting brief passages for the purpose of review, no part of this publication may be recorded, reproduced or transmitted by any means, including photocopying, without the written permission of Veloce Publishing Ltd. Throughout this book logos, model names and designations, etc, have been used for the purposes of identification, illustration and decoration. Such names are the property of the trademark holder as this is not an official publication.

Readers with ideas for automotive books, or books on other transport or related hobby subjects, are invited to write to the editorial director of Veloce Publishing at the above address.
British Library Cataloguing in Publication Data – A catalogue record for this book is available from the British Library. Typesetting, design and page make-up all by Veloce Publishing Ltd on Apple Mac. Printed in India by Replika Press.

Preface

Equality is in, and women these days consider themselves the equals of men in all domains: politics, business, high level sports, artistic creation, etc. In *'Le Fou d'Elsa,'* Aragon had predicted that woman would be the future of man, and perhaps the third millennium will prove him right? Yet, already in 1903, the first woman racing driver was about to emerge: Camille du Gast. Others followed. Rising to the call of adventure, they took risks in order to reach the top. Few succeeded … And yet exceptional women are often superior to 'exceptional' men!

Bravo Jean-François for this research work! This is a fascinating book, doubly so since this is a man paying tribute to the women!

They fully deserve this recognition.

Annie Soisbault
Marquise de Montaigu

Face powder, lipstick and racing tyres

Since time immemorial, there have been regular instances of exceptional women whose sporting skills have matched and surpassed those of the men. As we are about to discover in this book, the world of competitive motor racing – dominated as it is by men – is no exception, even if male resistance to these new women racing drivers was frequently fierce. Fortunately, this was fairly soon brushed aside!

The first of the women racing drivers, Frenchwoman Camille du Gast, was banned from racing by the Automobile Club de France after her Paris-Madrid race in 1903, on the grounds of 'feminine excitability'! A woman of some character, she consoled herself with motorboat racing in the open sea, between Algiers and Toulon, where she almost drowned.

On the English circuit of Brooklands, women were to be excluded from racing until 1908. Even then, they were only allowed to race each other in Ladies' Cups; the reason given: there was no such thing as a lady jockey! Despite this, England was to prove one of the best breeding grounds for women racing drivers: the highly glamorous Kay Petre, always in pale blue overalls; Elsie 'Bill' Wisdom; the blonde Eileen Ellison, and the infamous Fay Taylour.

Soon, with the end of World War I, new careers were evolving in numerous sports disciplines throughout Europe and the United States: speed-track records for Gwenda Stewart-Hawkes, the woman with three husbands; endurance raid rallies and the Monte-Carlo Rally for Mrs Mildred Bruce; places of honour in Grand Prix for the curvaceous and smiling Hellé Nice and her Bugattis; the infamous Violette Morris, an all-round top level athlete, and winner of the 1927 Bol d'Or, who was on the receiving end of a hail of Résistance bullets after joining the Gestapo ...

Back in France, the women – many of whom had taken part in the Le Mans 24-Hour races before the war and until 1951 – had to wait for the 'Women's Lib' of the 1970s, the beautiful blonde, Marie-Claude Beaumont, making a comeback at Le Mans in her muscular Chevrolet Corvette after being refused entry several times. Was the Automobile Club de l'Ouest (ACO) – the Le Mans racing governing body – being cautious or chauvinistic?

It was not long before Europe was to provide a rich variety of circuit and rally races, though it is noticeable that, the further south you go towards the Latin countries, the longer one had to wait to see very many women racing drivers of a high standard!

But let's get back to the beginning. At the end of the 1890s, which saw the advent of the industrial age and construction of the first motorcars, the winds of change were blowing. Women had gained certain legal rights and "working married women were to be allowed to dispose of their income as they pleased"! A not insignificant detail, since – in France, at least – in order to drive and race a car, a driving licence was necessary, which required proof of ownership of the vehicle that was used for the test.

So, at the beginning of the 1900s, more and more women were passing their driving tests: "Apart from the physical pleasures derived, driving gives women the means of expressing themselves and discovering their fitness for autonomy," said Alexandre Buisseret in *Le Mouvement social*.

As the pages of this book will reveal, for these intrepid new women – whether propelled by luck or driven by perseverance – to have access to the wheel of a motorcar, a few essential conditions had to be met: a certain amount of wealth, total freedom of movement, and, most of all, a sturdy disposition. The women concerned were motivated in different ways: for the Duchesse d'Uzès and Camille du Gast, premature widowhood; for Hellé Nice, witnessing the extraordinary vision of the first Paris-Madrid cars racing past her when she was a little girl, holding her teacher's hand; for Hélène Delangle, emancipation through high level sport for Violette Morris, a surviving World War I ambulance driver; a millionaire husband who was passionate about motorsports for Lucy Schell; and a horse winning at 20:1 for Victoria Worsley. All of these women were to use the dawn of the motorcar to help them direct, affirm and manage their lives. Racing was to procure for them recognition in an essentially masculine world, with the addition of a sensational bonus: panache and universal admiration!

Some of them attained glory or met with tragic ends, others retired to start a family at the peak of their careers, or sometimes simply disappeared, forgotten, into destitution. But one thing is certain; this life of competition totally devoted to their passion provided – just as with their male counterparts – more than they could ever have dreamt of: a remarkable life.

As time and wars went by, races, records and rallies around the world became more organised and more professional. Cars were to get ever faster, but that same spirit of tenacity that drove generations of women racing drivers, from the least known to the most illustrious, was to endure, even if, at the time of writing, there are no women to take over from Maria Teresa de Filippis, the first female Formula 1 Grand Prix driver in 1958; followed by Lella Lombardi in 1975; Divina Galica in 1976; Désiré Wilson in 1980, and Giovanna Amati in 1992.

One last remarkable fact: France gave women the ultimate major trophy: Michèle Mouton, World Rally Vice Champion in 1982.

To all women.
To those in my family who bore with me until the end of the book.

1

A new century, and the infancy of motorcars and petrol engines. Thanks to Dunlop and Michelin, wooden wheels were being fitted with tyres, and speed was on the increase. From being regarded as merely a means of transport that would replace the horse and carriage, the automobile soon became a vehicle of modernity and speed. The development did not escape the notice of Europe's great capitals, whose automobile clubs, in a unifying surge and in a bid to attract public attention, decided to organize great long distance, city-to-city races. These first trailblazing 'cannon-ball runs' were to herald the start of great motor races.

And the role of women in all this? A woman was represented rather like a figurehead on the early manufacturers' allegorical posters, or else mocked and criticised as a lost figure that had accidentally strayed into this brand-new mechanical universe. She was planted at the wheel of a hackney cab, or depicted changing a wheel. Nanny even drove motorised perambulators, but this was intended more to cock a snook at modern times, or to create a souvenir postcard. Some women, however, were to go further ...

The very beginning

1900

Full speed ahead for two stylish ladies in their Berliet Grand Sport, sparking the envy of the young dandies in the barouche.
(JFB Collection)

Right: A woman posing in the driver's seat, although it would have been impossible to actually drive wearing a hat like that! (JFB Collection)

Far right: Another 'figurehead' female driver, somewhat stiff-looking, and still with an unlikely hat. (JFB Collection)

A female taxi driver, broken down. A 'real' one, with cap. (JFB Collection)

Right: Two confident-looking English girls, out for a good time. "Out of the way! The two of us are having fun, speeding!" (JFB Collection)

Far right: Cartoon from the famous satirical English magazine, Punch, shows a motorised perambulator race in Kensington Gardens. Nanny No 18 is the fastest! (JFB Collection)

Bertha Benz (1849-1944)

If Frenchwoman Camille du Gast was really the first female racing driver to take part in a major international event, tribute must also be paid to Bertha Benz, the dynamic wife of engineer Karl Benz, and in 1888, generally credited as the first woman to drive a motor vehicle solo.

In the early hours of an August morning, while her husband was still sleeping, she undertook a journey of 180 kilometres (111 miles) from Mannheim to Pforzheim. Although not a race, it was against the clock to arrive before dark at the home of the grandmother of her two children, aged 14 and 15 years – whom she had taken with her, without her husband's knowledge! Meanwhile, Bertha had had to repair the leather drivebelt at a village cobbler's shop, unblock a carburettor pipe with a hatpin, refill the tank with ligroïne (petroleum ether) at a pharmacy, and – the height of eroticism – insulate the only electric ignition cable with one of her garters. On their arrival that evening, the three conspirators sent a reassuring telegram to the head of the family, who was verging on the hysterical.

Another female contribution to this fledgling marque – the daughter of Emil Jellinek, the Austro-Hungarian consul and commercial partner of Karl Benz and Gottlieb Daimler – was named 'Mercedes.'

Anne de Mortemart, Duchess d'Uzès (1847-1933)

On opening their newspapers one spring morning of 1898, Parisians learnt that "on this 23 April, Madame the Duchess d'Uzès passed her driving test."

At 51, attired in her inevitable black hat, and accompanied by three examiners from the prefecture, at the wheel of her brand-new 2-cylinder Delahaye she progressed from the statutory 12km/h (7.5mph) in inner Paris to an average of 20km/h (12.5mph) in the Bois de Bologne. "It would be wise," advised one journalist, "not to entertain any ideas of taking the family out for a drive."

Getting out of her car, the duchess noted with satisfaction that women had just surmounted a new barrier. She could not have spoken a truer word: just as she did when out hunting, our new driver displayed the utmost verve. On 9 June, barely a month and a half after obtaining her licence, whilst driving with her son amongst numerous carriages on the Avenue du Bois de Bologne (currently Avenue Foch), she was whistled down and arrested by a policeman. This was to be the first case of speeding; over 12km/h in town, for which transgression she had to pay a five franc fine – the maximum. The wheels of justice were already turning …

This woman, who subscribed to the progress of her era, was (as well as bringing up her four children, a (failed) political involvement supporting General Boulanger in his efforts to restore the monarchy, and being involved in feminism) to found the first female Automobile Club in 1926. With the Comte de Rohan-Chabot, she went on to organize the celebrated Paris-Saint Raphaël Rally. She even drove her entourage to Rome, where the rally was to be blessed by Pope Pious XI, and was received by Mussolini.

Although the duchess had opened up the way, the number of driving licences issued to women barely reached 100 before 1914. After the war, there was still

Bertha Benz. The dynamic wife of Karl Benz. In 1888, she drove 180km (111 miles) between Mannheim and Pforzheim with her two children. (Daimler-Chrysler archives)

The Karl Benz 1888 Patent Motorwagen, a single-cylinder, two-gear tricycle, being filled with ligroïne at the pharmacist on the day of Bertha Benz's famous trip. (Daimler-Chrysler archives)

2-cylinder 6CV Delahaye Type 1 Break, in 1897. The vehicle is preserved intact in the Château de Compiègne museum. (JFB Collection)

The Duchess d'Uzès, a very capable woman, famous for her hunting, and as much at ease on a horse as in a car. She was the first woman to obtain a driving licence, at the wheel of her Delahaye Break, on 23 April 1898. She was also responsible for the first case of speeding. (JFB Collection)

The Avenue du Bois de Bologne in Paris (now the Avenue Foch) was a fashionable spot for a drive during the Belle Époque. There were plenty of people about at 10:15am on that day, 9 June 1898, when the policeman issued the duchess with a fine. She had exceeded the statutory 12km/h (7.5mph) and incurred a 5 franc fine! (JFB Collection)

much debate over whether or not a woman's place was at the wheel – let alone at the wheel of a racing car! A few female attempts to participate in automobile events were later reported in the press: Mrs Laumaille completed a Marseilles-Nice in 1898, Mrs Labrousse a Paris-Spa in 1899 (coming in fifth in a field of male competitors), and the Contessa Elsa Albrizzi in a Benz at Padua – but did these count as real races?

Camille du Gast (1868-1942)

Suddenly it happened! Can you imagine a woman at the wheel of a racing car? This was certainly the unanimous cry of the press when Camille du Gast, 'the amazon with green eyes,' and 'the Valkyrie of the motorcar,' finished 33rd out of 122 participants in the great 1901 Paris-Berlin race, onboard her immense Panhard-Levassor. Very shortly to become the widow of Jules Crespin, manager of the Dufayel department store in Paris, our intrepid amazon threw herself into extreme sports of every kind: mountaineering, parachuting, fencing, and luge. Quite fearless, she acquired a passion for motor racing, supposedly after an affair with James Gordon Bennett, founder of the eponymous cup and owner of the *New York Herald*.

At the time, Camille du Gast was depicted as an elegant, handsome woman with an imposing and nonchalant beauty. Her wealth, her magnetism, her independence, and her gallantry were often the talk of the town, and her totally unprejudicial attitude was often to attract the jealousy of the motor sports authorities. She was later alleged to have had numerous love affairs, and even (wrongly) accused of having posed nude for the painting of *La Femme au masque* by the fashionable painter Gervex. This scandalous woman was unsettling in an age when a woman at the wheel was almost immoral!

In 1903 she set off in the great Paris-Madrid race to the applause of a delegation of sportswomen, and with a kiss on the hand from the Marquis de Dion. It was four in the morning and this was the start of what would be a chaotic race – unbeknown to the 207 participants, for some of whom dust, overtaking, humpbacked bridges, level crossings, and speeds approaching 75mph (120.7km/h) were to turn this sporting outing into a calamity.

Beyond Poitiers, the heat got the better of the competitors: blinded by dust, a Mors smashed into a Darracq; a Brouhot ploughed into the crowd, and Barrow's De Dietrich swerved to avoid a dog and hit a tree. Marcel Renault, blinded by the dust from Théry's Decauville, missed a bend and overturned. He died two days later. Meanwhile, further on at La Combe-sur-Loup, Camille du Gast, who was among the leaders, met with the horrific sight of Stead's overturned De Dietrich on top of its driver, who was crushed beneath the steering wheel. She immediately stopped and rushed to his aid. Thanks to her and the onlookers who ran to the scene and lifted off the wrecked car, Stead was saved from certain death. A sign of things to come? It was in Camille du Gast's nature to come to the rescue, and she went on to found dispensaries for teenage mothers and destitute women. Most notably, she was to become

Camille du Gast, the first woman racing driver, posing in bloomers, the sporting attire of women cyclists, invented by a female American journalist. Tightly corseted, our future racing champion has a hand's span waist. (JFB Collection)

Place de la Concorde. A flag meeting takes place in front of the headquarters of the Automobile Club de France in 1899. Camille wears an admiral's hat and full dress uniform. The driver (standing) wears a sardonic expression. (ACF archives)

1901 Paris-Berlin Race. Competitor No 122, Camille du Gast at the checkpoint in her 20CV Panhard-Levassor, with her elegant mechanic, the Prince de Sagan. In her first race, she finished 30th out of 154 competitors – all male. (ACF archives)

Camille du Gast and the Prince de Sagan on their Panhard, at a checkpoint in the Paris-Berlin race. (Ventugol Collection)

president of the Society for the Protection of Animals, founded by Gordon Bennett in 1903.

With the Paris-Madrid race aborted in Bordeaux and the forlorn racing cars sent back by train, Camille decided to take part in the 1904 Gordon Bennett Cup, which was set to run between Berlin and Paris. But the German press waxed indignant: a woman at the wheel? Considering the recent carnage of the Paris-Madrid, the ACF sports commission decided to exclude Madame du Gast for reasons of inexperience and 'female excitability!'

Disappointed by so much arbitrary inflexibility, but not defeated, Camille du Gast then threw herself into powerboat racing. She piloted the Marsouin, a Darracq motor racer, at the Juvisy meeting in 1904. Attired in a long constricting dress and captain's hat (with violet), before a large crowd she carried it off, according to the press "with some gallantry"!

Encouraged by this start, in May 1905 Camille took part in the open-sea Algiers-Toulon race. In the lead, but caught in a tremendous storm in which all of the competitors either abandoned ship or sank, she was rescued *in extremis* by the destroyer *Kléber*, and was declared the winner two months later!

Also a highly experienced horsewoman, she crossed the length and breadth of the Moroccan desert on horseback. However, strangely enough, it was her daughter who put an end to this adventurous life. A jealous and mercenary individual, she had been trying for a long time to extort money from her famous mother. By the skin of her teeth, Camille escaped an assassination attempt, instigated by her daughter's ruffian friends, at her home in the middle of the night. She confronted them and they turned tail and fled. Faced with a daughter who had deceived her, nothing was ever the same for Camille after that, and from that point until her death in Paris in April 1942 she devoted herself to her beloved animals. In her memory, a street in Ménilmontant bears her name: Rue Crespin-du Gast.

Right: 1903 Paris-Madrid race. Competitor No 29, Camille du Gast, at the weigh-in at the Place de la Concorde, checking the oil level in her still immaculately white Dietrich 35CV. (ACF archives)

Far right: The splendid Dietrich 45CV at the finish in Bordeaux, 76th out of 97 classified. If Camille had not stopped to rescue Stead, she would have been placed eighth! The board fixed across the top of the radiator indicates the size of the front axle. (JFB Collection)

1903: Camille du Gast trying the Benz Parcifal beside Marius Barbaroux, the French engineer and driver hired by Karl Benz to develop his motors. (Daimler-Benz archives)

Far left, top: September 1904, and a water sports meeting at Juvisy, with Camille du Gast at the helm of the Darracq-powered Marsouin. (ACF archives)

Far left, bottom: The crowd throngs onto the quays of the port of Juvisy. (ACF Archives)

A proud Camille du Gast before the start of the race, dressed in a long coat, hat, gloves and veil. Elegance and concentration prevail. (ACF archives)

The races continued and so did the women. The disciplines multiplied. Jeanne Hervaux was incredibly successful in hillclimbs, and climbed the Ventoux in a 4-cylinder Werner, as well as racing at Deauville, Château-Thierry, Gaillon, and Laffrey. At an exhibition at the Crystal Palace in London, she performed a 'looping-the loop' display in a car, but, from 1910 began a new career in aviation after obtaining her pilot's licence in a Blériot. She even opened a flying school for women – an enterprise that was to fail for lack of candidates.

Jeanne Herveux. Racing driver and pilot. (JFB Collection)

Jeanne Herveux at the start of the Ventoux hillclimb in 1907, in a four-cylinder Werner. She was the first female to race in the event, completing it in 47 minutes. (Louche Collection)

Dorothy Levitt

France was not the only country to produce women racing drivers. In England in 1902, Selwyn Edge, director of the Napier company and famous racing driver (he had won the Gordon Bennett Cup that same year), spotted Miss Dorothy Levitt amongst his staff, a beautiful secretary with long legs and eyes like pools. In a bid to promote his cars – and no doubt having found other hidden qualities in her – Edge decided that she should take part in a race, though first he had to teach her to drive. She surpassed his expectations by winning her class in the 1903 Southport Speed Trial, and proved such a good racing driver that she was taken on by Dion for a major publicity stunt. At the Hereford Thousand Miles Trial in 1904, Dorothy posed before

Dorothy Levitt at the wheel of her Gladiator, after her class win at the 1903 Southport Speed Trial. She was the first English female racing driver. (DR)

members of the press, delighted by her uncommonly glamorous racing outfit, holding a snappy Pomeranian dog that barked ferociously at all the other competitors – who got their own back the following day by sporting hideous toy dogs attached to their bonnets during the races …

In 1906, Dorothy broke the ladies' speed record by reaching 96mph (154.5km/h), and also achieved a remarkable time in a Napier at the Shelsley Walsh hillclimb. But Dorothy Levitt's participation went largely unnoticed until her victory on the Brighton seafront, where she proved just how well she could handle an enormous green 80hp works Napier. Encouraged by this success, Napier sent her with the works team to race in the Herkomer Trial in Germany, which she completed easily with no penalties, and still in the most incredible outfits! Since women were banned from the brand-new Brooklands race track, she followed the Napier team in France and successfully took part in the Gaillon hillclimb race before vanishing from the sporting scene.

Her extravagant racing outfits aside, Dorothy Levitt is considered to be the first English female racing driver.

Ethel Locke King (1864-1956)

At the beginning of the 19th century, every country had grasped the economic importance of the burgeoning automobile industry. In England, in order to develop and promote it, a rich landowner from Surrey who had been to the Coppa Florio races in Italy decided, with backing from the British Car Owners' Association, to create a new venue where the great marques could

Napier en route to Brooklands. (B Brulé Collection)

compete against each other, which he hoped would be a showcase for English technological supremacy. The Brooklands circuit, with its banked bends, was born (or almost!). The first sod was turned in August 1906, but after a year of intense work, during which the cost increased tenfold, King was practically ruined and on the verge of a nervous breakdown.

King's rich and industrious wife, Ethel, daughter of the powerful Governor of Tasmania, Sir Thomas Gore-Brown, came to his rescue by raising the necessary funds (£150,000) to finish the work. She inaugurated the circuit, leading the procession at the wheel of her Itala with her husband at her side.

If the Brooklands track was saved thanks to a woman, officials of the Brooklands Automobile Racing Club (BARC) failed to recognise this when they decided to ban the lovely Dorothy Levitt and her green Napier from racing, citing the fact that, as there were no lady jockeys, why should there be female racing drivers? Feelings ran high in the press, but the officials remained resolute.

In 1908, the ruling was relaxed a little and a race was prepared especially for women: the Ladies Bracelet Handicap. Dress included coloured outfits and scarves, and participants tied cords around their bodies to hold up their skirts. "It would have been very improper to show one's knees aboard a car that was already stripped of any bodywork and which could not have hidden anything!" Of the eight women racers, Muriel Thompson's Austin won ahead of Ethel Locke King and her Itala.

Although the spectators were enthusiastic, the BARC officials were less so, still refusing to mix the genders until the 1920s, when women racers still had to have a male mechanic as a team-mate. But the wheels of destiny were turning, and many of these daring women served their country by driving ambulances at the Front. Those four years of war in Europe served as a springboard for several of these future women racing drivers, enabling them access to a sport that was initially only available to the well-off.

Hugh Locke King, the husband of Ethel, to whom we owe the Brooklands track. (DR)

Selwyn Edge and Dorothy Levitt's works Napiers. (DR)

2

Bobbed hair
in fashion

1920

The war was over, and nothing would ever be the same again. Those who had survived had a new philosophy of life, and racing was slow to get back into the swing. Meanwhile, a new generation of women racing drivers was about to emerge. During the conflict they had been ambulance drivers, taxi drivers, lorry drivers and, occasionally, military motorbike couriers. This was the case with Violette Morris, an all-round athlete and future Bol d'Or champion. Similarly, at the exit to the chain of Unic factories in Puteaux, the test drivers were … females. The 'Lionnes' (lionesses) were light of foot and had a keen ear, and, above all, they drank less than the men! At Brooklands, racing did not begin again until 1922, once the damage to the track caused by an Air Force Station had been repaired. The United States had created Indianapolis, Berlin had the nearby Avus, and Italy had Monza, but France still had no track for testing its high-powered racing cars. Fortunately, the Montlhéry track was to appear in 1924, followed by that of Miramas, near Marseilles. For the next twenty years these circuits were the Mecca of Grand Prix meetings and speed records for motorbikes and cars – and even aeroplanes.

An unknown beauty at the Bois de Bologne on the front of her Alfa Romeo 3-litre RL Super Sport, wearing her hair short and kitted out in a Grand Sport jump suit. (JFB Collection)

oreover, to re-launch a motor industry ruined by the war, a 1920 law – the 'Le Troquer' act, named after its minister – was to launch a new type of economical vehicle – the cyclecar – that even became a way of life for many. The basic design was a capacity of 1100cc, a weight of 350 kilos, and a maximum of 2 seats, from which emerged the Amilcar, BNC, Morgan, Salmson, and Benjamin, which were very much sought-after by young French women racing drivers such as Mesdames Depret, Schell, Hellé Nice, Bourdeneau, Versigny, Mertens, Leblanc, and many others.

They cut their hair, used Houbigant 'Fougère Royale' perfume, wore cloche hats, and learnt to drive so that they could obtain their 'brevet,' as the French driving licence was called in those days. There were even driving schools for women, and the Duchess d'Uzès and the Comte de Rohan-Chabot enrolled them in their women's automobile club to take them rallying across Europe! Hurrah for the Roaring Twenties!

There were those who took the sport very seriously: for some, this would lead to glory, but for others, shame …

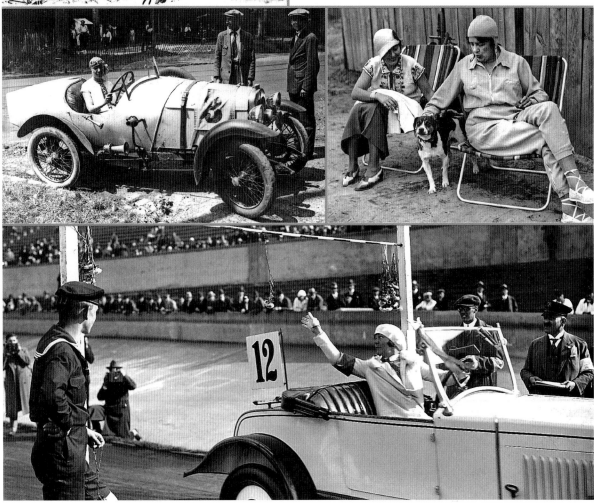

Learning to drive. Ladies' driving school: that's reassuring, it's a 'chic' school.
(Prévot Collection)

L'Automobilia, 1928, an illustrated bi-monthly journal. (JFB Collection)

A machine at the service of the well-groomed woman. Little cars with small engines become popular. France took to the motor car and women became emancipated. (JFB Collection)

Once emancipated, the women formed societies. The l'Automobile Club féminin de France magazine was founded in 1926 by the Duchess d'Uzès, and produced by the Vicomte de Rohan-Chabot. On the death of the duchess, the torch was taken up until the war by the Duchess de Gramont, Mrs André Citroën, the Princesse Galitzine, Mrs Schneider, Mrs Deutsch de la Meurthe, Mrs Mareuse, Mrs Grégoire-Sainte-Marie, along with several others. (Archives patrimoine Renault)

A tomboy, Violette Morris was brought up in a convent, where she soon displayed great talent for sports and PE. Duly trained from the age of fifteen, she became junior boxing, swimming, football and running champion; water polo, the Libellules team, weightlifting, and javelin – she did it all. She also boxed against the fearsome Lucienne Velu from 1912 to 1935: "Whatever a man can do, so can Violette!"

In 1914 war was declared, her new husband left for the Front, and her boxing club was transformed into a Red Cross station, all of which prompted Violette to sign up. She took her driving test and found herself at the wheel of an ambulance in the hell that was Verdun, but was demobilized and sent back to Paris after falling sick.

Then came the end of the war and the stadiums re-opened. Violette Gouraud-Morris celebrated her 27th birthday and went on to shine at the Paris Olympics. She made quite a name for herself with her victories in the javelin and shot put in the first female Olympics in Monte Carlo. With her contacts in motorbiking and cyclecar circles – and thanks also to her cycling successes in Buffalo and the Vél d'Hiv – she had the good fortune to be offered a Benjamin cyclecar for the 1922 Bol d'Or. Her mentor, who had considered this a publicity stunt only, was surprised by her fourth place and lap record. A fortnight later, she won the tough Paris-Pyrenees-Paris race. Then, in 1923, in the Paris-Nice and still in her

Violette Morris, 'the hyena of the Gestapo' (1893-1944)

Violette Morris earned her stripes as a driver on the slopes of the Somme in 1916. On roads potholed by shells, she dodged the craters on her motorbike. On several occasions, she fell in the mud, whereupon, without a word, the French soldiers, or poilus, would help her to right her machine. Little did they suspect that her shapeless outfit concealed a woman who was to win the famous Bois de Saint-Germain race: the 1927 Bol d'Or!

1928 Bol d'Or in the forest of St-Germain. Violette Morris sets off in the lead, in her BNC cyclecar. (JFB Collection)

Violette Morris at home, surrounded by souvenir photos of her speed trials at the Vél'd'Hiv, her BNC racing car, her female conquests, and her husband, Cyprien Gouraud. (Bavouzet Collection)

Violette even sang light-hearted songs, such as a revival of the Mistinguett hit, Fleur d'Amour. *In this photo she still has her breasts, though not for much longer. Her boxing gloves can be seen hanging over the frame above the piano. (Bavouzet Collection)*

Benjamin, she won her class – the team cup, the women's cup, and that of the President of the Republic! She re-entered several years in a row.

For all that, the now-famous 'la Morris' did not abandon athletics. Despite smoking three packets of American cigarettes a day, and by now heavier, with massive thighs, muscular neck, and the shoulders of a removal man, she was even known to use her fists during football matches: people did not mess around with her! Her misdemeanours began to mount up on her dossier with the French women's sporting federation. Her three-piece men's suits and indiscretions with her friends in the changing rooms also raised eyebrows. In 1927, she was refused a licence for wearing the same masculine suit, but this fooled nobody, as she never really hid her homosexual nature.

Disappointed at not being able to take part in the 1928 Olympic games, she devoted herself entirely to cars, and opened an accessory shop at the Porte de Champerret in Paris. She hit the headlines yet again by having her breasts removed – a double mastectomy like the legendary Amazons – to prevent being obstructed by them at the wheel of these super-fast cars.

The following year was marked by a spectacular lawsuit, for Violette Morris appealed against the federation's refusal to grant her a licence. A malicious press crammed into the court, only too happy to blow out of proportion the story of this outrageous woman who mixed with the Parisian elite, and who frequented the Caf' Conc' with Joséphine Baker, at the piano, singing the Mistinguette song Fleur d'Amour, or even walking the boulevards in a pearl grey suit and floppy felt hat, cigarette dangling from her mouth. Despite the oratory performances of her lawyer, Maître Lot, her case was dismissed. To add to her misery, the 1929 crisis loomed, which did nothing to help small businesses, including that of the unfortunate Violette. She was saved from bankruptcy by a racing contract with BNC cyclecars.

It was during this period of crisis that – still haunted by the Stavinski affair – she met a former racing rival, Gertrude Hannecker, a journalist from Germany, who was, in fact, a recruiting agent for the SD Nazi – the Nazi Security Service. The die was cast … She was received with much pomp and circumstance on Hitler's official VIP stand at the 1936 Olympics in Berlin where, along with

In 1929 Violette Morris appealed against the removal of her sports licence. Here, she awaits the verdict with her lawyer, the famous Maître Lot. Her case was dismissed. (Bavouzet Collection)

five other former foreign celebrity athletes, she received a medal from the German sporting authorities, which moved her; in this country, at least, her past sporting achievements were recognized. So, she gradually rallied to the Nazi cause "... for France to finally leave behind its decadent bourgeois parliamentarism and form, alongside the Reich, a bloc of progress and hope for young people, based on friendship and a longstanding peace."

Armed with these connections and her sporting prestige, which opened many doors for her, she went on to betray secrets to the Nazis: Maginot Line layouts, lists of telephone exchanges, and even the plans for the new Renault-Somua tank. In the clutches of the SD, she became a spy. Although she slipped through the net of the French counter-espionage services, the English were alerted, and the Special Operations Executive began to compile a dossier on her.

In March 1939, Hitler annexed Austria and the Sudetenland. Yet, during this period of turmoil, the French quietly carried on with their lives. With a lower profile now, Violette scraped a living giving driving and tennis lessons. Paris fell in 1940, and German troops moved in, along with the Gestapo. The notorious Gestapo headquarters in Rue Lauriston were formed, which was where Violette Morris was to be found, taking advantage of the black market: to transport hams and Bollinger, drivers were needed! Moreover, always ready

with a punch when instructions had to be enforced, 'la Morris' went down very well in the underworld (a subject very well documented by Raymond Ruffin in his book about her).

Spotted by Lafont, she soon rose in the ranks of the French Gestapo, the 'Carlingue.' But bureaucracy was also slow in Germany, and it was not until 1942 that the SD found Violette Morris again. Given her past motoring and Parisian experience, she was put in charge of dismantling terrorist resistance movements. Using brutal interrogation, machine guns, and seduction of female pupils that she had 'educated,' she was regrettably effective against the Résistance fighters. Amongst others, she brought down the English network of 'automobilists' led by Charles Williams-Grover and Robert Benoist, famous Bugatti Grand Prix racing drivers. Benoist only just managed to escape by jumping out of the Traction that was taking him to the Rue des Saussaie. Williams-Grover and Norbert Mercier, a Peugeot racing mechanic, were not so lucky ...

The 'hyena of the Gestapo' as she was known, ended up seriously ruffling feathers in London, and a commando operation was mounted against her. In an ambush by the Normandy Resistance, she died at the wheel of her supercharged '15' under a hail of machine gun fire. Exit 'la Morris' with her 20 national titles, 50 medals, 200 football matches, and three Bol d'Or races.

BP-Energol advertisement. Violette Morris was a famous role model in the racing world. (JFB Collection)

'La Morris:' men's clothes, 'clope au bec' and 'godasse de plomb' – 'dangling fag' and 'leadfoot.' (Bavouzet Collection)

Violette Morris' business card. (Binda Collection)

Violette Morris and her co-driver, Mrs Lefèbvre in a George-Irat. (JFB Collection)

Start of the 1937 ladies' Paris-Saint-Raphaël in front of the ACF headquarters in the Place de la Concorde. (JFB Collection)

Montlhéry, 2 June 1929. La Morris wins the skills contest in her BNC cyclecar. (Hebert Collection)

Hellé Nice, a dancer at the Casino de Paris in 1928. (Bavouzet Collection)

Montlhéry, 2 June 1929. Hellé Nice posing beside her Omega 6, unaware that she is about to win her first race. (Bavouzet Collection)

Hellé Nice, the Bugatti queen (1900-1984)

Eccentrics are determined to conquer and win: fortunately, they were not all like Violette Morris. Instead of longing to be a 'circus rider' like other girls, the young Hélène Nice knew that she wanted to be a racing driver. She was standing at the side of the road watching the Paris-Madrid racing cars dash past in the sunshine and dust on a May morning of 1903, in the Beauce region, to the south west of Paris. As Louis Renault was the first to pass by amidst a swirl of gravel and the smell of hot oil, followed by a certain Camille du Gast, Hellé gripped the hand of her school teacher very tightly – but at the age of three, would she remember all that she saw?

Hélène Delangle (Hellé Nice was her stage name) had big blue eyes and a wide smile with dazzling white teeth, an image that earned her her first dancing contract at the Casino de Paris. After a difficult start, posing for some 'saucy' fashion photos, and some nocturnal encounters with eager admirers, she at last launched into Parisian life.

With her earnings, she bought her first car in 1920: a small Citroën. This was the start of a great love affair with all things mechanical which was to change her life. One fine day, in a car accessory shop in the Rue Saint-Ferdinand owned by Henri Courcelles,

a former ace pilot in the First World War, she met the young Philippe de Rothschild. All three were to become the very greatest of friends. While at the Brooklands racetrack, where Courcelles was working on a broken-down Grégoire, there was nothing else to do but watch the race. This was a revelation for Hélène, by now Hellé Nice, who, at that time, was moving in high society between Deauville, Nice, Italy and Mégève. A great sportswoman, she even climbed Mont Blanc. Courcelles entered the Le Mans 24-Hours in 1923, in a large Lorraine-Dietrich, coming eighth overall.

Hellé Nice clearly had a strong yearning to try motor racing for herself, after receiving a few lessons from Courcelles, so she jumped at the chance of doing some publicity for the Omega marque by taking part in the third all-women's Grand Prix race at Montlhéry on 2 June 1929. Facing serious competition from the likes of the American, Lucy Schell (BNC), the favourite;

Mrs Ferrand (Amilcar), and, above all, the fearsome Violette Morris (Donnet), she crossed the line 100 kilometres (62 miles) later in first place. First race, first victory! Her disarming smile beneath her big bright blue eyes promoted Ettore Bugatti to proclaim "The perfect match for the colour of my Bugattis," and he entrusted her with a Type 35C Grand Prix to attempt the record on this track at Montlhéry. Elisabeth Junek had stopped competing after the death of her husband at Nürburgring, and Hellé was certainly a possible replacement as the marque's 'face.' So Nice's motoring career was launched, and she gave up dancing and the Casino de Paris.

During the course of the love affairs and friendships that would provide her with cars, she drove some extraordinary models all over the world – Alpha Romeo, Monza, Bugatti 35C, supercharged Miller and Duisenberg – and mixed with high society. In town, she drove a Hispano. In 1930, she spent six months

Hellé Nice (Bugatti No 62) in the 1931 Dieppe Grand Prix, with Lord Howe (Delage 1500, No 34). (Mouchoux Collection)

Hellé Nice came eighth at the Comminges Grand Prix on 26 August 1934 in a 2.3-litre Alfa Romeo 8C Monza. (Raffaelli Collection)

in the United States and raced on every track on the East Coast, followed by ten years of partying, speed, sex, drink and all-consuming passion. But, as for any shooting star, there is an end. 1936 was to be an ill-fated year in every respect for Hellé Nice. Escaping from economic recession and strikes, she was invited to take part in Brazilian Grand Prix racing. There, in São Paulo, she suffered a terrible accident that destroyed her Alfa Monza and left her in a coma for several days. She received considerable financial compensation from the Brazilian government, but her life had changed, and so had the world around her. After setting a spectacular

promotional record for Yacco oil with female colleagues Claire Descolas, Odette Siko and Simone des Forest, she was sidelined, the bouts of amnesia that she suffered as a result of her accident making her a bad risk at the wheel.

However, in 1938 she drove a German DKW in the Chamonix Rally with the famous womanising Baron Huschke von Hanstein, who was chiefly known for his success with BMW, and in the Thousand Miles under the Nazi propaganda colours. Following a breakdown during the rally, their spare time became a brief idyll in the mountains.

On 6 August 1939, she won her last race in a small family Renault Juvaquatre at a promotional rally in Comminges. Three weeks later came mobilization and the outbreak of war, putting an end to any sporting activity. During those war years Hellé Nice disappeared from the limelight, though seen in Arcueil and then in Nice in a sumptuous Juan les Pins villa.

After liberation, life slowly returned to normal. Still in contact with Anne Itier, she decided to enter the 1949 Monte Carlo rally with a small 4CV Renault that she had bought in Nice. On the evening of the opening gala, a dramatic turn of events proved disastrous to her career: into the midst of all her racing friends – Yvonne Simon, Germaine Rouault and Anne Itier – came Grand Prix ace Louis Chiron, accusing her of having been a Gestapo agent during the war! Shocked, she made no reply, but the damage was done and doubt and rumours were rife. Her former liaison with Huschke von Hanstein in 1938 perhaps made Chiron – to whom she had never yielded – jealous.

Amongst her meagre possessions after her death, a photo was found of a German officer in full uniform; Friedrich Leopold von Richthofen, the air army general. He had sent her his get-well wishes after her terrible accident in São Paolo in 1936. No charge was ever found against her, and the mystery remains unsolved. The one thing that is certain is that this was the start of a long, slow isolation that was to separate her from the motoring world, which was all that she knew. Ruined and abandoned by her last partner, she was taken in by the charity 'La Roue tourne' (on account of her dancing career). She was to die in utter destitution in a squalid garret in Nice in 1984. So, did she have a secret?

Jill Scott

Luckily, not all our women racers met with such a dramatic end. Accidents were common, of course, but not all were fatal; more often than not, races were exciting and happy occasions for all. There were even racing couples; for example, William Berkeley 'Bummer' Scott and his wife drove their racing cars as a family.

Jill Scott was the wealthy heiress of a coal empire, and the couple lived in a large house next to the Brooklands track, where they spent most of their time. Shortly after their marriage, the pair bought a Sunbeam Indianopolis, followed by several Bugattis. All of their cars were painted black with emerald green wheels. Jill and Scott won many trophies with their Bugattis, but this was not enough for them. After the accident that killed the hapless Parry Thomas in the enormous Thomas Special 'Babs,' with its 27-litre V12 Liberty engine, they bought two of his other cars: the famous

Thomas 'Flat Iron' and a Leyland Eight. Jill only just managed to reach the pedals of these two monsters, but this did not prevent her from crossing the 120mph (193km/h) barrier, which bestowed the right to affix the famous 'Brooklands 120mph badge' – so sought-after by collectors nowadays – on one's radiator grill.

Even their five month old baby daughter was allowed a lap at 100mph (161km/h) on Jill's knee as Scott drove their brand new Sunbeam GP!

Like her colleague, Mildred Bruce, Jill Scott also flew her own Avro Avian plane. It was perhaps because of this second passion that, one fine day, she fell in love with Ernest Thomas, a former RAF pilot, and divorced her husband. Thomas was also a member of the BARC and, with Jill, continued to monopolize the victories at Brooklands in Alfa Romeo and Frazer Nash respectively. They lived happily together for many years, until Jill passed away in 1974 after a peaceful life.

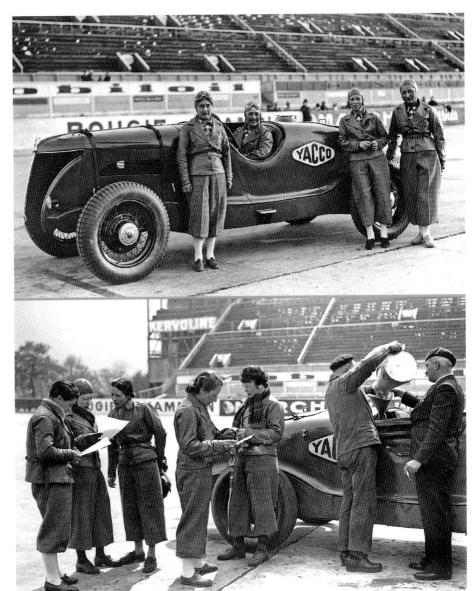

Top: Montlhéry, 19-28 May 1937. The Yacco record for 30,000km (18,641.14 miles) at 140.88km/h (87.54mph) for Hellé Nice, Odette Siko, Claire Descolas, Fernande Roux and Simone des Forest. Ten world records were about to fall at once! The Matford-Yacco was called 'Claire.' (JFB Collection)

Above: A pre-record briefing from 'Brown Owl,' Claire Descolas. (JFB Collection)

Right: Brooklands, 1928 and Miss Bond's damaged Bugatti. She escaped unhurt after hitting the barriers at 150km/h (93.21mph). This is learning the hard way! (JFB Collection)

Far right: Jill Scott at Brooklands in July 1928 at the wheel of her Sunbeam Indianapolis. (JFB Collection)

The famous Brooklands banking during the Kent Short Handicap race. Birkin's Bentley overtakes Jill Scott's black and green Bugatti and Jack Dunfee's Ballot. (JFB Collection)

Jill Scott in the brand new Leyland Eight in 1928. (Bavouzet Collection)

J G Parry Thomas' 'Flat Iron,' the Leyland-Thomas No 1. The 'Flat Iron' was bought by Jill and 'Bummer' Scott after Thomas' death at Pendine Sands. In the photo is George Duller, another famous Brooklands racing driver and former jockey. (JFB Collection)

Victoria Worsley

Unlike the Scotts, not everybody could afford to compete at Brooklands, Montlhéry, or in the Alpine Cup!

Victoria Worsley, who earned a modest living of £2 a week as her father's chauffeur, had the good fortune to win at the races. Thanks to her brother's lucky wager, she won at 20:1, and left the York racecourse with enough to buy her first car – a Salmson Grand Sport!

After some encounters and a few exchanges, she ended up with an MG which she was able to enter many Ladies' races at Brooklands, with her brother as passenger or team manager, in accordance with the local anti-female regulation. Victoria was one of the 'faces' of Brooklands between 1928 and 1932. She married a member of her team, who became head of timing at the Crystal Palace circuit.

Victoria Worsley filling up her MG Midget on 9 May 1930, at the start of the Brooklands 24-Hours race. (JFB Collection)

Victoria Worsley, sporting broad smile, elastic around the ankles, scarf, hair band and 'goggles.' Although this was May, it was about to pour with rain. After a faultless race, she finished seventh in her class and 20th overall. (JFB Collection)

Joan Chetwind (?-1980) and May Cunliffe (?-1975)

Despite aggravation from the BARC, more and more women took to the track. Joan Chetwind made a name for herself by beating the 12-Hour record at an average of 133.5km/h (82.98mph) in her Lea Francis. She was related to Henry Birkin, one of the 'Bentley Boys,' victors at the Le Mans 24-Hours. For a long time, she was the long-distance record rival of the Hon Mrs Victor Bruce, and it was also she who gave advanced driving lessons to the beautiful, blue-eyed Dorothy Stanley-Turner, the future famous MG motor racer.

May Cunliffe, despite being an excellent racing driver, was not as lucky in her career. An unfortunate accident in 1928 on the sandy track of Southport Sands beach resulted in her passenger, her father, being crushed when her Sunbeam overturned after failing to negotiate a bend. She had, nevertheless, made a remarkable debut at the age of twenty in a Bentley, with which she broke the women's record at Shelsley Walsh in 1926. She raced one last time in Shelsley and broke her jaw in an unlucky crash whilst crossing the finishing line.

She also had her pilot's licence, and drove service vehicles for the US Army throughout the war, after which she bought another large Dodge 4x4 for her personal use. She even test drove Kieft Racer 500s during the 1950s.

Joan Chetwind beating the 12-Hour record on the Brooklands circuit with her Léa-Francis 1500, and grabbing a quick cup of tea. (JFB Collection)

Above right: Southport Sands, in 1928. May Cunliffe and her father aboard the Sunbeam Grand Prix, just before the fatal accident. (JFB Collection)

The Sunbeam skidded on the sand track and crushed May Cunliffe's father. Although assured of a fine sporting career, she retired and turned to a career in aviation.

Mildred Bruce (1895-1990)

The Honourable Mrs Victor Bruce; her venerable husband's title always opened doors for her. He worked at AC cars and had just won the 1926 Monte Carlo Rally in appalling snowy conditions. She was the only daughter of Lawrence Petre, the owner of Coptford Hall, and an American mother who was a Shakespearean actress. Her grandmother had lived through the gold rush and fought the Indians; no need to look any further for the origins of Mildred's mischievous and sturdy character. At fifteen, she was already driving all the county's policemen up the wall on her brother's motorbike!

Passionate about motorsport, she obtained a new car from the AC factory in order to enter the 1927 Monte Carlo with her husband, where she won the ladies' cup after spending several consecutive hours at the wheel. On reaching Monaco, and with the factory's agreement, she decided to continue southward with the same car for an endurance test, crossing Italy, Morocco, Gibraltar, Spain, and France, then off to Montlhéry for a quick spin of 1000 additional miles (1609km), eventually returning to AC at Thames Ditton. This was a massive publicity coup which established the couple's reputation as globetrotters.

That same year she set off again on a trek to the Arctic Circle to plant a British flag. In December, she and her husband took on a 15,000 mile endurance record with their gallant little 2-litre AC on the Montlhéry track – ten days and ten nights of cold and snow. Victorious but exhausted, the whole team then escaped a fire in their hotel in the Chateau Montlhéry by the skin of their teeth – one of the mechanics had fallen asleep in his bed with a lit cigarette! Meanwhile, 17 records had been well and truly broken. She returned to Montlhéry in 1929 with a massive 4.5-litre Bentley 'Blower,' and beat the 24-hour record at 89.4mph (143.89km/h). She would have done even better had she not taken a large gulp of petrol from a Vichy bottle during a refuelling stop …

Mildred Bruce never wore racing overalls. Always elegant, she raced in a jacket, pleated skirt and pearl necklace. "I'm not a liberated woman," she declared. "As a youngster, I was one girl against five brothers, and I've always tried to hang on to my femininity."

Victor Bruce posing amongst his 1926 Monte Carlo Rally trophies, which he won with his 2-litre AC (having started from John O'Groats in northern Scotland). In 1927, at the beginning of a long career, his wife won the ladies' cup and finished sixth overall. (JFB Collection)

The Honorable Victor Bruce, M Stevenson, and their AC during the 1926 Monte Carlo, somewhere in the snow in Scotland. They won the rally a few days later. (JFB Collection)

Mrs Mildred Bruce, a beautiful, petite redhead with mischievously sparkling eyes. She became the ladies' pre-war endurance champion of road, track, sea, and in the air. (Getty Images)

She was to race at Brooklands and again at Monte Carlo before deciding to tackle records on the water and in the air. Mildred bought a biplane – the Bluebird – and, after forty hours of flying, decided to chance a solo round-the-world flight! After several breakdowns and forced landings, she reached Tokyo and returned to London. The fame she acquired after this flight gave her the idea of founding her own aviation company in Croydon; Air Dispatch.

Mildred was to secure other records around the East Indies and China. Ever dynamic, she created a regular service between London and Paris before the war. She was also the first to use an air hostess – Miss Daphne Vickers – aboard one of her planes. During the Battle of Britain, she flew a plane by night for Defense Contre Avion training (where she trailed a blimp for trainee gunners to shoot at), and raced horses by day. On top of that, she developed a factory for repairing planes for the RAF, which was to earn her a fortune!

After the war, she retired to Bradford-on-Avon, where she led a quiet life, surrounded by her parrots and her favourite racing cars. She renewed her pilot's licence for one last time at the age of 80 and performed the loop-the-loop. She passed away at the remarkable age of 94; like a cat, she appears to have enjoyed each and every one of the nine lives predicted by her mother.

Victor and Mildred Bruce in the ice and snow during their attempt on the 15,000 miles (24,140.16km) record at Montlhéry, 9-19 December 1927, a two-driver relay at an average of 68mph (109.5km/h). Crazy! (JFB Collection)

The Honourable Mrs Victor Bruce at the wheel of her 4.5-litre Bentley Blower. She had just beaten the solo record for 2000 miles (3218.7km) in 24 hours. This was on 7 June 1929. She was glad to be able to return her car intact to the Bentley factory, as she needed to use it again a few days later in the Le Mans 24-Hours, with Earl Howe and Bernard Rubin. Mildred's record stands to this day. (JFB Collection)

The poster for Brescia Week in 1921. (DR)

Racing was also moving on apace in the rest of Europe, each country having its circuits and its champions. In Italy, the Baronessa Maria Antonietta Avanzo won the women's cup at the Brescia Week festival in 1921. As the papers enthusiastically reported, it was to forget an unhappy love affair that she threw herself into racing so wholeheartedly and successfully. As a Venetian, she would have preferred powerboat racing but this wasn't fast enough!

Pilot, journalist and confirmed racing driver in Italy, she was to appear during the 1930s in Alfa Romeos, Maseratis, and Bugattis on circuits, in the Rocca di Papa hillclimb, in the Mille Miglia, at Le Mans, at Indianapolis in a Miller in 1932, and even in the Tobruk-Tripoli in 1940! She had numerous rivals: Jole Venturi (OM); Corinna Braccialini (Alfa 1500); Anna Maria Peduzzi, who raced from the 1930s to the 1950s and was nicknamed 'Marocchina' – or 'Moroccan Girl' – for her attractive skin tone, and Dorina Colonna, a bewitchingly beautiful Roman princess. She entered the 1930 Mille Miglia with Romeo Formenti in a 1750 SS Alfa Zagato, but was foiled within a hair's breadth of the finish.

Other racers included Germans Edith Frisch (Bugatti) and the countess Einsiedel in a Bugatti at the Targa Florio, more French women, still in Bugattis, Mesdames Siko, Mareuses, Jennki, Albertine Derancourt (who allowed her eight-year-old son to drive), Emma Munz in Switzerland, and even in Czeckoslovakia, the famous Eliska Junkova, better known as Elisabeth Junek.

Dorina Colonna in the 1930 Thousand Miles with Romeo Formenti, in Alfa 1750 SS. (DR)

Below: Jole Venturi in the 1931 Thousand Miles, in an OM. (DR)

The Baronessa Maria Antonietta d'Avanzo, at the wheel of her 1921 Alfa Romeo ES Sport. (DR)

Champion of Brescia Week, the Baronessa Maria Antonietta Avanzo. (JFB Collection)

Mrs Versigny in a Bugatti at the St-Germain hillclimb in 1928. (Brulé Collection)

1934 Alpine Cup. Edith Frish and her mechanic, Karl Treber, en route to Munich in a 2-litre Opel. Her challengers were Claire Descolas in a Bugatti and Lucy Schell in a Delahaye. (JFB Collection)

Albert, the son of Albertine Derancourt, a Bugatti Grand Prix driver. She was very proud of him. (JFB Collection)

Elisabeth Junek, queen of the steering wheel (1900-1994)

Born in Olomouc in the heart of the Austro-Hungarian Empire, Elisabeth was the sixth daughter of a village blacksmith, with little likelihood that, one day, she would become a Bugatti Grand Prix racing driver. A gifted linguist, who learnt German and English, she landed a job in a bank, where she met her future husband, Cenek Junek.

In 1921, fortune smiled on them, and Cenek Junek began to race. In 1922, Elisabeth took her driving test in secret and obtained a racing licence: this was the beginning of the Junek team. The pair bought a Mercedes and their first Bugatti Type 30, which Cenek gave to Elisabeth. Bugatti maintained a link with her, and she went on to become Ettore Bugatti's favourite. All their Bugattis bore bright yellow livery at Elisabeth's request as she had stood transfixed by the colour of a clump of buttercups in front of the steps to the Chateau Saint-Jean in Molsheim when taking delivery of one of their Bugattis.

Her first victory came in 1925 at Zbraslav-Jiloviste with the ex-Strasbourg Grand Prix 2-litre Bugatti: her career had taken off. She successfully competed in hillclimb races in Czechoslovakia, Germany, and at Klausenpass in Switzerland, her triumphs making her a national hero.

Encouraged by this wave of success and by the Bugatti marque, Elisabeth entered the 1927 Targa Florio in Sicily with a Type 35B. After two laps she abandoned the race with steering failure; a pity, as she was fourth! She decided to return to Sicily for the 1928 Targa, with another brand new Type 35B. This was to be the finest race of her career. In the lead on the second lap, ahead of the other great works racing drivers such as Chiron, Divo and Campari, she compensated for her lack of strength by having spent days and days memorising the 1500 bends of that Targa Florio, only losing her lead after a burst water pump which relegated her to fifth place – a truly fantastic performance, when all is said and done. This race made her a legend.

Sadly for her, two months later, her husband, who was racing in the German Grand Prix in Nürburgring, left the road and was killed instantly. Although at the height of her fame, she was utterly devastated and decided to retire from racing and sell all their Bugattis. She consoled herself by returning to her former love, which was travel, moving to the island of Ceylon (now Sri Lanka). Ettore Bugatti gave her a Bugatti with which to promote the company in Asia.

Elisabeth Junek remarried shortly after the war and found brief happiness again before the Iron Curtain fell on her, as she had returned to Czechoslovakia. Luckily, our queen of the steering wheel was to live long enough to see the fall of communism and be able once again to visit all of her 'Bugattiste' friends the world over as guest of honour. Some legends live forever ...

Below right: Elisabeth Junek at the Klausenpass in 1926 with her Bugatti 35, named 'Otakarkem.' She was first in the ladies' cup and second in class. (Nicolosi Collection)

Elisabeth Junek and her Bugatti 43 on Charles Bridge in Prague, during the summer of 1929. (Nicolosi Collection)

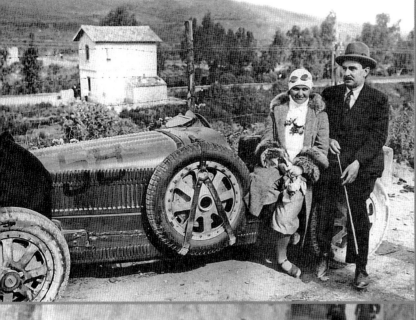

Top left: Elisabeth Junek and the Chevalier Florio. (Brulé Collection)

Above left: Targa Florio, 6 May 1928. Elisabeth Junek, in her Bugatti 35B, was fifth overall after a fantastic race that made her a legend. Her husband, Cenek, was killed two months later at Nürburgring. She then stopped racing. (Nicolosi Collection)

Elisabeth Junek on a visit to England, with Rivers Fletcher (BRM) on her right, and Mike Spence (Lotus). (JFB Collection)

Top right: Targa Florio, 1927. Elisabeth Junek sitting on the front of her Bugatti 35B.

Above: Targa Florio. Junek in a Bugatti in 1928. (Nicolosi Collection)

3

Things get serious …

1930

Events became more numerous and more specialised, though the same was not necessarily true of our racing drivers as this was still the age of 'gentlewoman drivers.' Our valiant amazons began the season with a Monte Carlo Rally, then appeared in a Grand Prix or at Brooklands, taking in the Le Mans 24-Hours and a little Paris-Saint Raphaël amongst friends! Others went off on a world tour, as did Miss Darthys and M Lacor with their Delage in June 1929. Might the crisis, caused by the Wall Street Crash, have carried them off without a trace? There is no mention anywhere of triumph or failure! A convoy of eight Czech women left Prague for a trek to Morocco in Aerosport cars: Prague-Frankfurt-Paris-Marseilles-Bône-Biskra-Touggourt-Algiers-Casablanca-Marrakesh. Quite an itinerary. Judging by the photo, this must have been so they could set up a cactus plantation …
During this between-war period, the automobile industry was flourishing and even flamboyant, with stiff competition between Hispano, Delage, Bugatti, Delahaye, Amilcar, Talbot, Bentley, Daimler, and Mercedes.

Setting off from Prague, a procession of eight Czechoslovakian women, at the wheels of their Aeros, about to cross Europe and North Africa, heading for Marrakech. The situation was obviously fairly prickly, given the cacti attached to their wings! (JFB Collection)

From Prague to Marrakech, 14,000 kilometres (8699 miles) in an Aero. (JFB Collection)

Azur guides and Michelin maps. (JFB Collection)

Miss Odette Darthys and M Lacor bound for the world tour with their Delage. Departing from the Place de la Concorde and duly checked in by the AFC, did they actually arrive anywhere? (JFB Collection)

Car manufacturers from every country in Europe vied to conjure up ways of promoting their image. For a long time women had been used on posters to sell products, but featured even more so now behind the wheel of a car; this advertising was so successful that women also became car buyers!

Music hall stars, musicians, genuine racing drivers, aristocrats and members of the 'upper crust' were invited to compete in events; any meeting or rally was an excuse to have fun and potentially promote the marque that did the inviting. The Paris-Deauville Rally was the favourite of stars and starlets, and 'Parachute' rallies entailed collecting up as many small bags of ballast – which had been dropped by planes – as possible. Dubonnet flowed at the dinner in the Dauphine Pavilion, and prizes were donated by the department stores of Le Louvre, La Fermière in Vichy, Rodier, Lactéole, and Chocolat Menier, whilst a gramophone was graciously lent by the house of Electrope.

In 1933, Peugeot organized Women's Days at Montlhéry featuring 301 races. All of the great names of the Monte Carlo Rally and Saint-Raphaël were there – Mrs Hustinx, Mrs des Forest, Hellé Nice, Mrs Mareuse, and Mrs Siko.

For others, speed was taken really seriously. The Montlhéry track was not rented out to amuse the crowd, but for real records in 'men's cars:' Gwenda Stewart-Hawkes, Kay Petre, Joan Chetwynd and Hellé Nice were there to prove this.

At Brooklands, Ethel King took over the running of the BARC after the death of her husband, and lifted the ban on women racing. Henceforth, from 1927 women were able to race cars without having to take a male with them, or deal with male antagonists, of which Kay Petre was a victim when she was accidentally rammed in a race by Reg Parnell's MG. Reg was deprived of his licence for a year, but, nevertheless, had a fine post-war career in Formula 1 with Ferrari, BRM, Cooper, etc.

Setting off on the artists' rally for Deauville, from the Sacré-Cœur in Montmartre. (JFB Collection)

Paris-Deauville artists' rally. 'Cruising along.' (JFB Collection)

A Parachute Rally near Paris, with the Aéroclub de France. (JFB Collection)

Mrs Hustinx, des Forest, Mrs Marinovitch, M Sénéchal. (JFB Collection)

Serious stuff, timing. (JFB Collection)

Top: Miss Betty Vlasto, breeder of Borzoi hounds. Who most resembles whom? (Bavouzet Collection)

Above: Ladies' days at Montlhéry, during the summer of 1933, involved drivers such as Hellé Nice, Marinovitch, des Forest, and Hustinx racing Peugeot 301s over 25km (15.5 miles). (JFB Collection)

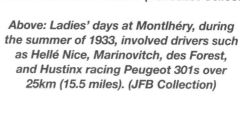

Gwenda Stewart-Hawkes, the thrice-married racing driver (1894-1990)

As with Violette Morris, the war had been the making of Gwenda Stewart-Hawkes. No ambulance driver could match her at avoiding shell craters. The daughter of a Major in the Royal Engineers Corps who had fought in the Boer War, she was a chip off the old block. Her own passion was for speed records. She began racing with motorbikes and moved on to cars. As Brooklands was hit by a ban on night use because of noise, Gwenda was obliged to find another track, and did so in Montlhéry.

The famous Brooklands fishtail exhaust was very fashionable elsewhere in Europe, though in Britain was not a stylistic affectation but an obligation because of irascible neighbours, who even complained that strawberries from a kitchen garden tasted of petrol!

Gwenda had been married to Colonel Janson, director of the Spyker car company, but the marriage was short-lived, and it was with a new husband, Colonel Neil Stewart, that she set off for France and for Montlhéry. She established a new world 24-hour motorbike record with a Terrot-Jap, despite leaving the track spectacularly several times. The couple converted one of the rooms at the speed track and spent several months there, awaiting favourable weather conditions to make record attempts. That marriage was also not to last, as she had an affair with one of her mechanics, Douglas Hawkes, who had 'supported' her during her records, and who became her third and final husband.

Douglas Hawkes directed the Derby engine and car company. This was a significant boost for Gwenda, as he brought her the famous Miller Special from the United States, which had been designed especially for the Indianapolis races. Like the Derby, this was a front-wheel drive car. A Miller with a record-holding woman at the wheel – what an excellent way to guarantee publicity! The car was prepared by Derby and became a Derby-Miller, shattering several one-mile speed records at the Montlhéry oval between 1930 and 1933. And she nearly 'went out with a bang': crossing the 140mph (over 210km/h) record finish line, she landed in the circuit barriers.

Gwenda raced twice in the Le Mans 24-Hours, driving a Derby (of course!) sport and a Derby with a Maserati engine, but without great success. Her expertise lay purely in breaking speed records. In 1940, the couple returned to England to join in the armament effort. Douglas had a mechanical engineering factory at Brooklands, and Gwenda worked at making shells for the duration of the war. Afterwards, they set sail in their yacht and spent a year cruising the Greek islands, and

Gwenda moved permanently to the island of Poros in order to lead a quiet life. Upon the death of her husband in 1974, she made several journeys across Europe and cheerfully drove back to England in her little Citroën 2CV. She passed away in 1990 at the age of 96.

Gwenda Stewart-Hawkes at the wheel of an ERA at Brooklands in 1937. (JFB Collection)

Gwenda Stewart-Hawkes at Montlhéry at the wheel of her record-making Derby-Miller, in May 1933. (Bavouzet Collection)

Gwenda Stewart-Hawkes in the 2-litre Derby-Miller, which broke the mile and kilometre records at over 234km/h (145mph) in 1933 on the Montlhéry oval. (JFB Collection)

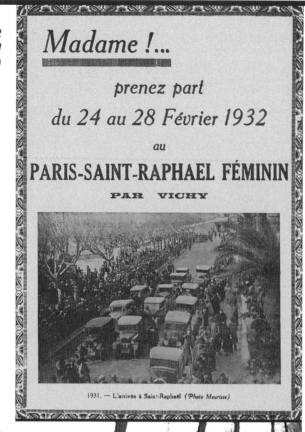

Madame !...

prenez part
du 24 au 28 Février 1932
au
PARIS-SAINT-RAPHAEL FÉMININ
PAR VICHY

1931. — L'arrivée à Saint-Raphael *(Photo Meurisse)*

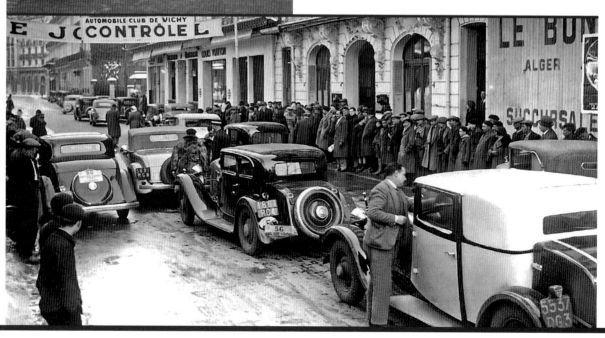

Lighthearted and serious at the same time, the ladies' Paris-Saint-Raphaël Rally had been created by the Duchess d'Uzès in 1929; its technical director was the Comte de Rohan-Chabot, and the organizer was the Automobile Club du Var. These ladies (exclusively) regularly took part in a long rally that set off from Orly (there was no airport in those days) and descended on the Côte d'Azur, in four days and three stages, via Nevers, Vichy, Lyons, Saint-Étienne, and Grenoble (at the Croix-Haute mountain pass, chains were graciously lent by the Grenoble tourist board). Then came the sunshine and the Napoleon Route, via Sisteron, Manosque, Marseilles, Toulon, Fréjus, and Saint-Raphaël. At the finish, flowers, celebratory wine and a banquet would await them. It's all in this February 1932 rally programme. In the group photo, they are all wearing cloche hats. It would have been considered unseemly for them to go out bare-headed or 'en cheveux,' as the French said at the time. Over the years, regulations became more sophisticated, and the weights of passengers (and animals) were taken into account. There were sectors for speed and gymkhanas. This rally, just like the Monte Carlo Rally and the Tour de France automobile, was to survive the war and serve as a benchmark for future great women champions such as Annie Soisbault and Michèle Mouton.

Meanwhile, it was all of the crème de la crème of the world of rallies, the Parisian upper crust, and English sportswomen, who disported themselves in February on the French roads: Mrs and Misses Mareuses, Friedrich, Descolas, Schell, Hustinx, Radisse (the cellist), des Forest, Riddell, Marinovitch, and even highly fashionable pilots such as Amy Johnson.

January 1931, a brief stop at Grenoble. A snowman and the 'Comte de Rohan-Chabot' (beret and scarf), surrounded by Mrs Radisse, Mrs Marinovitch, and many others. (JFB Collection)

The rally in Auvergne ... (JFB Collection)

... and in the Alps. (JFB Collection)

Right and below: In the snow, wearing town shoes, a lovely 'Rally' Grand Sport roadster. (Bavouzet Collection)

Talbot 'DD' in the snow. (Bavouzet Collection)

Renée Friedrich, the daughter of the Bugatti
dealer in Nice, with her Bugatti 44, in 1931.
All went well that year. (Nicolosi Collection)

Simone des Forest and her 4CV Rosengart, at the
Paris-Juan-les-Pins. (JFB Collection)

Paris-Saint-Raphaël, 1938.
Regulations called for car
and driver to be weighed.
A severe test for the
ladies! (JFB Collection)

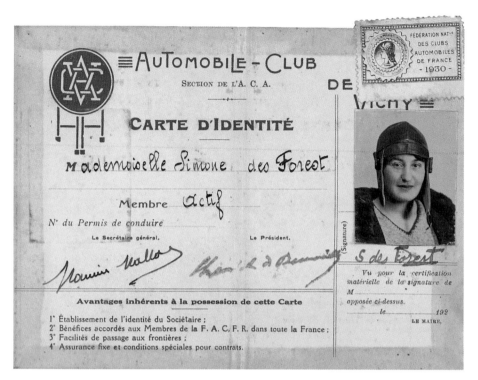

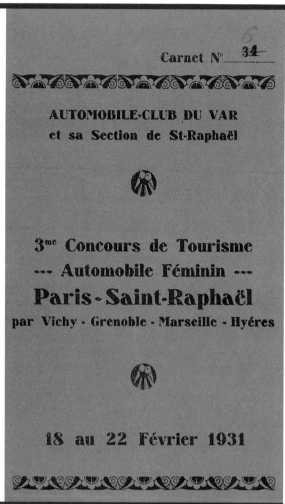

AUTOMOBILE-CLUB DU VAR
et sa Section de St-Raphaël

3ᵐᵉ Concours de Tourisme
--- Automobile Féminin ---
Paris - Saint-Raphaël
par Vichy - Grenoble - Marseille - Hyéres

18 au 22 Février 1931

Licence and time-card book.

Below: The Rosengart 4CV in action during the Fréjus Plage 500m sprint race. She won the first category of the 1931 Paris-Saint-Raphaël. (JFB Collection)

Lucy Schell and her Bugatti 44. Paris-Nice, 1930. (Bavouzet Collection)

Top: Mrs Deutsch de la Meurthe in a Hispano Binder. 1930 Paris-Saint-Raphaël. (Brulé Collection)

Middle: Mrs Rouault and her Delahaye, winner of the 1936 event. (Brulé Collection)

Bottom: Mrs Paindavoine and her Bugatti 43. (Brulé Collection)

Above: Adjusting the make-up is the order of the day at the end of the first stage! (JFB Collection)

Above, right: Picnic pose with charcuteries provided by Olida for Lucy Schell's works Delahaye 135.

Paris-Saint-Raphaël Rally in 1934. The AFC administrative checks. Mlle Hustinx, M de Cortanze and two officials. (JFB Collection)

Start of the 1938 Paris-Saint-Raphaël at the Place de la Concorde. The chefs of the great Parisian restaurants distribute picnics to the competitors. (JFB Collection)

The administrative and technical checks took place with a certain bonhomie in front of the Automobile Club de France and the Hôtel de Crillon in the Place de la Concorde, where rally plates and picnic hampers were distributed by the chefs of the great Parisian restaurants, before departure with the blessing of the Duchess and the comte. The first checkpoint was Orly, en route to Nevers.

Just before Nevers, a large hill marked the start of the Pougues-les-Eaux hillclimb, which, in 1932, was to prove fatal for Renée Friedrich, daughter of the Nice Bugatti dealer. Just to please her, Ernest Friedrich, who had raced for Delage, agreed to let her take part in the splendid brand new D&S cabriolet. She skidded on a sheet of black ice and hit a tree, and only her mechanic, Robert Bourgeois, survived. The competitors met with storms and snow in February, especially after Saint-Etienne and Grenoble, but fortunately the outcome of the rally was, for the main part, a happy one, ending in a Concours d'Élégance in front of the Grand Casino in Saint Raphaël.

Furs, an MG and a gleaming rally plate. It's 'Next stop, for these English girls the Côte d'Azur!' (JFB Collection)

From left to right: Mrs Williams, Mr Hoore, Countess Möy, Miss Haig and Miss Ridell, on 14 February 1938. (Brulé Collection)

A pause during the 1934 rally, and a fine view of the rear of the Bugatti 43 Grand Sport. (JFB Collection)

Renée Friedrich in front of her Delage D8-S cabriolet, at the Porte d'Orléans. The 1932 Paris-Saint-Raphaël Rally. (Cabart Collection)

Renée Friedrich refuelling her Delage prior to her fatal accident on the Pougues-les-Eaux slope before Nevers, in 1932. (Cabart Collection)

Start of the 1932 Rally, greeted by the Duchess d'Uzès and the Vicomte de Rohan-Chabot. That year, the Duchess directed her troops to Rome, where the procession was to be blessed by Pope Pius XI and Mussolini. (JFB Collection)

February 1931. Renault Primaquatre, passing through the Croix-Haute pass, at the Hôtel du Grand Logis. (Patrimoine Renault)

Below: On the menu: Sévigné consommé, fillet of sole Auto Club, aspic of foie gras from Périgord, Rouen-style roast Nantes duckling, new peas from Valescure, Paris-Saint-Raphaël bombe and petits fours. Great wines from the Domaine de la Croix, Saint-Estèphe grande cuvée, Mâcon 1926, Ayala Champagne, and liqueurs!

Finish of the rally at Saint-Raphaël. Concours d'élégance before the gala dinner at the Grand Casino, 2 February 1931. (Bavouzet Collection)

Fernande Roux at the Concours d'Élégance at the finish in Saint-Raphaël in 1934. (JFB Collection)

DINER DE GALA
OFFERT PAR
L'AUTOMOBILE-CLUB DU VAR
EN L'HONNEUR DES CONCURRENTES
DU
IIIᵉ CONCOURS DE TOURISME AUTOMOBILE FÉMININ
PARIS-SAINT-RAPHAEL

Above, left: Passing through Toulon, the race is almost over for these English girls in their Singer. It wasn't very warm on the Côte d'Azur in February 1935. (JFB Collection)

Above, middle: Pomeranian and Bugatti No 40 in the Place de la Concorde in 1933. (JFB Collection)

Above: Betty Stresa and her Simca 5, the smallest car in the event, 1939. (JFB Collection)

Fine crew on a Renault. Place de la Concorde, in front of the Hotel de Crillon in 1937. (JFB Collection)

Renault No 60's time-card book. (Patrimoine Renault)

Carnet N° **29**

AUTOMOBILE-CLUB DU VAR
et sa Section de St-Raphaël

3ᵐᵉ Concours de Tourisme
--- **Automobile Féminin** ---
Paris - Saint-Raphaël
par Vichy · Grenoble · Marseille · Hyères

18 au 22 Février 1931

Bottom right: Lucienne Radisse, with her Renault at the finish in Nice. Discreet musical promotion in front of the purveyor of pianos and gramophones. (Patrimoine Renault)

Paris-Juan-les-Pins Rally. Lucienne Radisse with her very fine Delage D8. (Cabart Collection)

Lucienne Radisse (1899-1997)

There were confirmed racing drivers … and there were celebrity racing drivers. Lucienne Radisse was one of the latter: a virtuoso cellist, a beauty, film star, pilot, and wife of a journalist. Following her first marriage, which gave her two sons, Lucienne Radisse, whose successful concert appearance led to her giving live wireless performances, divorced and then married an aviator who was none other than the son of the director of the Henri Busser orchestra. After a series of concerts and hits in the great Parisian concert halls, she set off on a world tour from 1930 to 1939: New York, where she took her driving test in a Potez and exceeded 150km/h (93.75mph) in a racing Hupmobile; Havana; New Orleans; Hollywood, where she made a film in 23 days (*Le Bluffeur*, with André Luguet), and Mexico, where she was attacked in the train by terrorist bandits). She flew with Mermoz to North Africa, and crashed in a French airmail plane in Spain: luckily, her cello remained intact and she was able to give a concert that very evening! She moved amongst show and musical circles, and was a regular at the Paris-Saint-Raphaël women's rallies (which she won, alone at the wheel of her little Renault), and the Paris-Nice, in a giant Delage D8. She used to rest on arriving in St Tropez, where she kept her boat. She rubbed shoulders with Arletty, Charles Vanel, Tyrone Power, Paul Morand, and Audouin-Dubreuil. She was a celebrity racing driver!

Interrupting her musical career during the war, she put her driving skills to good use in Red Cross ambulances. Afterwards, she went back to her cello career though was not above driving her beautiful cabriolet 203 in 1960s Paris. She passed away peacefully in the Place de Passy in her 98th year.

Amy Johnson (1903-1941)

Amy was the daughter of a fish wholesaler from Hull in Yorkshire. A rebel at school, she was rather a tomboy, which was to cost her a new set of teeth after a violent encounter with a cricket ball! After following more sedate studies at Sheffield University, where she obtained a degree, she began working as a secretary for a London law firm. Finding this uneventful life not entirely to her liking, it was seeing an aircraft taking off near her home that fired her imagination and led to her obsession with flying. Using her meagre savings she took flying lessons, but did not immediately show any particular aptitude. She nevertheless passed her test and displayed such enthusiasm that she became the darling of her flying club. In addition, she was a pretty brunette with a dazzling smile.

The 1930s needed something spectacular, and, thanks to the support of a pilot friend and some judicious sponsoring, she planned to beat the record for a solo flight to Australia. She managed her flight in her Gypsy Moth, 'Jason,' in 1930, although the record was not beaten. Nevertheless, her sponsors' enthusiasm and publicity made up for it and her career was launched. She was to make many more flights – to Moscow in 1931, Japan, and the United States in 1933. Everyone was fighting over her. Always on the lookout for publicity, events and big marques were desperate to use her, so, in 1938 she was invited to take part in the very societal Paris-Vichy-Saint-Raphaël Rally in a Talbot-Lago T150 Grand Sport coupé, specially prepared for her by Anthony Lago. She won the Concours d'Élégance, while Betty Haig took first place in the rally. She also took part in the Shelsley Walsh hillclimb in a BMW 328, and should have taken part in the Monte Carlo, but at the last minute was detained in England by her divorce from Jim Mollison – a creditable racing driver, but a heavy drinker – whom she had married in 1932. She did, however, drive a massive Bentley coupé in the RAC Rally, but her results were not earth-shattering, and it was more her personality and charm that wowed the public.

The outbreak of war cut short her motoring career and she contributed to the war effort by transporting RAF planes. Unfortunately, one January morning in 1941, she became lost in atrocious weather and crashed her plane into the Thames. Her body was never found. She was another to enter into legend.

Amy Johnson. (JFB Collection)

Amy Johnson and her bi-plane. (JFB Collection)

Top right: The Paris-Saint Raph' became a celebrities' rally: pilot Amy Johnson and her Talbot in 1938. She carried out numerous long distance flights between Europe and Asia, Moscow, New York and Tokyo. In 1941, she crashed into the Thames while delivering an RAF plane. (JFB Collection)

7<u>e</u> RALLYE AUTOMOBILE MONTE CARLO

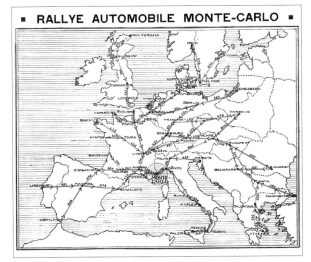

■ RALLYE AUTOMOBILE MONTE-CARLO ■

More serious and more testing for the mechanics and their drivers, the great Monte Carlo Rally had been going since 1911, though it was during the 1920s and 1930s that it really came into its own. The whole of Europe was fascinated by these competitors who set off on impossible routes in the height of winter, sometimes even in open vehicles, to find their departure point in the far reaches of the continent: Umeå, Tallinn, Bucharest, Warsaw, Constantinople, Gibraltar, Palermo, Athens, John O'Groats in Scotland, Rheims and Paris … Every year, there would be several women amongst the competitors. The path to the Ladies' Cup had been established in 1925 by Mrs Mertens setting off from Tunis in a Lancia.

The favourites of the 1930s, found in all the rallies of that time, were Vaughan, Mareuse, Schell, des Forest, Hellé Nice, Lamberjack (wife of the Bugatti dealer), Molander (famous for her victories in Saabs in the 1950s), Hustinx (who became Mrs de Cortanze), Marinovitch, Siko (she also raced the Le Mans 24-Hours), Rouault, Simon (with her little bunches), and Largeot. The cream of male racing drivers were also there, and these ladies did well to often come within the top ten in the overall rankings.

The English women in particular were never idle. Joan Richmond was the first woman to race in Australia, and, in fact, took part in the Australian Grand Prix in 1931 with her Brooklands Riley, then took two colleagues onboard, Jean Robertson and Kathleen Howell, returning by road in her Riley 9 to Europe, via Darwin, Malaysia, Bengal, Delhi, Alexandria, and Palermo in Italy. Joan then entered the Monte Carlo Rally which she finished a creditable 17th place in her class! She re-entered the following year, in 1932, with Kay Petre the Brooklands champion, but did not finish.

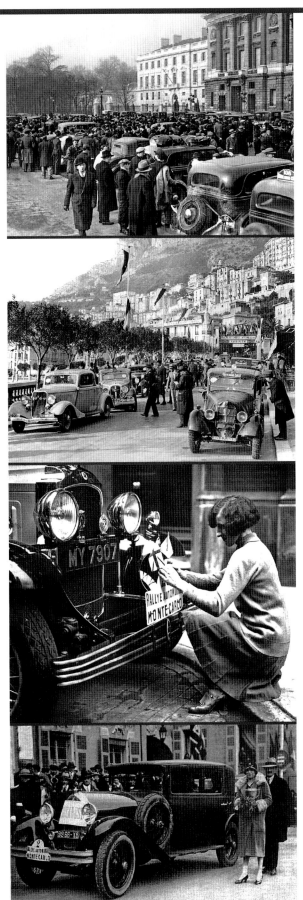

Far left: The 1928 concentration rally, which was almost won by Mrs Versigny, who started from Bucharest in her Talbot. A timing error at the end of the journey relegated her to third place, but did get her the Ladies' Cup. (JFB Collection)

Passage control at Place de la Concorde, in front of the ACF headquarters in 1934. Chains, cold, snow and mud … (JFB Collection)

… and the same at the finish on the port of Monaco. Pictured are No 8, Mrs Mareuse's 301, which left from Umeå and came third in the ladies' class, and No 93, Eck's Ford, and No 73, the Austin belonging to Bergan-Cederwal Larsen. (JFB Collection)

No 23, Mrs Dinsdale's 3-litre Vauxhall in front of London's Victoria Station on 20 January 1930, as she prepares to set off for John O'Groats in Scotland, her departure point for the Monte Carlo. She was to finish 48th overall. (JFB Collection)

Mrs Versigny and her Talbot. First of the ladies and third overall in the 1928 Monte Carlo. (Brulé Collection)

3am on 19 January 1931, and the Austin 21 belonging to Mrs Grave and Mrs Cleeve, at the start in Scotland. They finished 41st. (JFB Collection)

Bottom right: Route map. (JFB Collection)

Both pictures below: No 57 and three unknown competitors, lost in 'the middle of nowhere' in Central Europe. (JFB Collection)

28 January 1932, Mrs Vaughan and Mrs Naish won the Ladies' Cup in their Triumph, No 229, despite a prolonged stop whilst Mrs Vaughan – a doctor – treated a Danish competitor seriously injured on the road. This photo was taken at the finish, where the pair enjoyed a well-deserved cup of tea and cake. (JFB Collection)

1933 Monte Carlo. Mrs Gripper, Mrs Martin and Mrs Marshal sitting in front of their Hillman. They came fifth in the Ladies' Cup and 27th overall. (JFB Collection)

Mrs Mareuse and Miss Lamberjack, first of the ladies in 1933 with their little Peugeot 301. Art Deco stylishness is the order of the day. (JFB Collection)

Simone des Forest and Fernande Hustinx (1906-1994)

As a young girl from a good family, Simone lived in a country château in Gannat, in the Allier region of France. Her father was in the army. At twenty, she decided to set off with her friend, Fernande Hustinx, to conquer the snows of Central Europe and 'do their Monte Carlo.' Thanks to the complicity of Peugeot and their mentor, Charles de Cortanze, who was to prepare a 301 for them, the two young ladies were to go to Bucharest to take one of the official starts that scored the most points, but was also one of the most difficult. After a journey of 3772 kilometres (2358 miles) along dreadful, snowy roads, they made it back to Monaco and secured the 1934 Ladies Cup. Incidentally, it's thanks to Simone de Forest that this book came into being. By a stroke of luck, yellowing papers were later found in an old shoe box on a Rétromobile stand. A whole notebook of the route between Paris, Bucharest and Monaco, photos, and a few sketches, which had lain forgotten, told the story of Simone des Forest's past.

The Peugeot establishment did not have a model with sufficient capacity to compete against the favourites of the time for an overall win, so it decided to set its sights on the Ladies' Cup to show off its new 201 and 301 with independent front wheels. Cortanze organized a selection of female drivers at Montlhéry (a reminder of the ladies' days in Montlhéry in July 1933, with all those 301s lined up as though in a parade). Our two female rally debutantes had been selected there, and not

without some difficulty for the willowy blonde Fernande Hustinx: intimidated by the authoritarian Charles de Cortanze, she went too slowly in the first lap, and was almost excluded from the selection. She was braking too early, and, as examiner and passenger (already smitten?), Cortanze crushed her foot on the accelerator before every bend. With much screeching and jerking of the wheel, she achieved an excellent time! The Peugeot company had two identical 301s prepared, and Mr Charles de Cortanze personally served as chaperone for Simone and Fernande throughout the rally.

Departing from Paris at midday on 5 January 1934 with the objective of being at the Bucharest start on 20 January, 'Caroline' (a discreet tribute to Carol, King of Romania), Simone and Fernande's blue 301, closely followed by that of Charles de Cortanze and Gillard, headed for Strasbourg, with the intention of sleeping there. France was beset with snow and black ice; the forecast promised -25°C.

The following day took in Frankfurt, then Nuremberg. They had to drive on the grassy verge to achieve any grip in the freezing conditions. That night was spent at Nuremberg in a convent hotel with bibles on the bedside tables, then on to Prague and a 24-hour rest and general service for the two 301s – so far so good. Thermos and sandwiches were the order of the day, en route for Cracow – a tough leg. "This is where the real battle begins with the winter, the cold in all its forms, and the nature of countryside and towns changes. The costumes – dress coats – become

Fernande Hustinx, selected by Peugeot for the Monte Carlo. (Cortanze Collection)

Hustinx and Des Forest, winners of the 1934 Ladies' Cup in their game 301. They appear a little stiff, after travelling 3772km (2343.8 miles) of difficult roads since setting off from Bucharest. (JFB Collection)

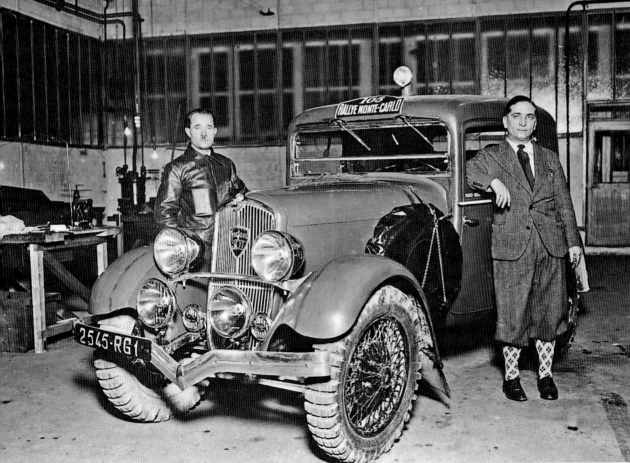

Cortanze and Gillard posing proudly before the start of the 1934 Monte Carlo, in front of their brand new model 301 with independent wheels. They were to chaperone (in every sense of the word) the Hustinx-Des Forest team to take them from Bucharest to the Ladies' Cup. Cortanze went on to marry Miss Hustinx. (Peugeot Archives)

3.772 Kilomètres

par deux Jeunes Filles

Simone des Forest's 1934 Monte Carlo logbook. (JFB Collection)

Five sketches from Simone's logbook.

Terrible blizzards and snowdrifts were experienced on the journey. (JFB Collection)

greatcoats. Pointed hats appear, sledges are pulled by long-haired nanny goats covered in frost from muzzle to tail. The road gets narrower and we come to mere tracks. Dense population. An old woman kisses the hand of Charles de Cortanze, promising him success and good fortune while chanting 'Dala, Rama, Macha, Talaaa'… He gives her alms. Warsaw is suffering from the severe cold. Snow and snowdrifts. We unpack trousers, boots and ski mittens. It's all white with frost inside the car. Our eyelashes are elongated by the frost … What with the wind, the holes and the 80cm (31.5in) snowdrifts, we shovel, and struggle to keep in the middle of the road. We meet some Dutch people who are also going to Bucharest for the start. Lwoy-Jassy, 528km (328 miles) in freezing fog that blinds us and forces us to drive with the windscreen open. We are alone, lost in these immense plains swathed in icy cotton wool. We come across sledges. They often get in our way, but sometimes help us. We harness some horses to pull Caroline, stuck in a snowdrift that was too deep." At Jassy, they shivered. At the hotels, even if the windows were double-glazed, there was only ever one blanket, and they did not shake off their colds until Monaco. A surprising encounter at the side of the road was a peasant leading a bear.

"16 January, Bucharest and its Automobile Club at long last. Colonel Lermite is all chivalry. Other competitors are already there: Berlesco and his Ford, a habitué of the route, some British and some Dutch.

"Set off again. Out of the sixteen who entered from Bucharest, we're down to seven. The rally has already exacted its toll. Today, 20 January, at 1:45pm, the road to Monaco is ours! And, before us, more snow, frozen plains, hamlets and, above all, the cold. Wolves? We haven't seen any (however, we do have a gun!). Our No 54 advances valiantly, slides along, skids and stops just in time. Luckily No 105 is not far away to help us dig our way out. First checkpoint: Lwoy. We are within the time limit. We take turns at the wheel. In Prague, there's just twenty minutes for a hot meal.

"First night on the road at Jassy, second in Warsaw. By the third night we had left Prague far behind us. On the 23rd, at six in the morning, we're in Frankfurt. Everybody's asleep at the Automobile Club – they weren't expecting us so soon. Short twenty minute nap, lying on the Club carpet! Set off again and remove chains. No more snow on the road. Soil, for the first time in three weeks. The little 301 goes like a dream. In the morning, we reach the conurbation of Strasbourg. The Athens contingency is already there. The Peugeot and Dunlop people are there. We get hugged. Well done, you deserve … a nice hot bath! Back again. Refuelling. Groups of cars are getting closer and closer together.

An encounter with a peasant and bear in Romania. Cortanze bravely shakes its paw. It's Miss Hustinx who is taking the photo. (Cortanze Collection)

Hustinx and des Forest in front of the big results board; they were seventeenth overall and first of the ladies. The flags on the roof represent all the countries they passed through. (Cortanze Collection)

Clockwise from top left:

1935 Monte Carlo. Des Forest and Siko, 36th overall and first in the Ladies' Cup in their Triumph. (JFB Collection)

Souvenir photo of the 1935 Monte Carlo Rally competitors, in front of the Prince's château. Miss Cotton sits at the wheel of her MG, and just seen is part of the wing of No 42, Mrs Hustinx's 301. (JFB Collection)

Letters from the Shell company, sponsor for the next (1935) Monte Carlo, where Simone des Forest was to win the 2nd category in a Triumph with Odette Siko. (JFB Collection)

Trévoux and Chinetti's Alfa Zagato, No 1, photographed by Simone on the ferry, at the start in Umeå, in Sweden.

Our morale is high. Game of overtaking with an old hand, a master of the route, Stoffel, No 126, also in a 301. Lyons during the night. General rally checkpoint, we meet up with those who started this morning, from the Place de la Concorde. Congratulations all round, bustling about, we get stared at. We're looking rather crumpled, my dear, and that's hardly surprising after 3250km (2019.5 miles) almost non-stop. Set off again. We soon shake off the nice, charming M Boillot, boss of Spidoleine oil. We put him in a panic. He's dreaming of his women's cup. Alternation of speed and feeling shattered. The sun finally rises over the Esterel massif. 24 January. As we approach, suddenly, in front of us in the middle of the road, a pedestrian who refuses to budge? In fact, it's a chap painting lines and numbers on the road. Swerve between the pots of paint and the fellow still bent over his paintbrush. Phew! Cortanze was really scared for us. Now he leads the way for us. Nice! Nearly there, and Monaco at last, our goal after 3772km (2344 miles). Flowers and kisses. It's over. Seventeenth overall and first of the ladies. Cortanze and Gillard are 16th, just ahead of us, with the satisfaction of a mission accomplished. Gathering for the prize-giving in the afternoon on the Rocher hillside, in front of the Prince's palace. Caroline has been washed for us, and regained her lovely blue colour. And what a beautiful silver cup!"

Simon des Forest and Fernande Hustinx went on to take part in many more rallies. In 1937, Simone, along with Hellé Nice, Odette Siko and Claire Descolas, beat a 30,000km (18,641 mile) record at Montlhéry in a Yacco Matford. Fernande became Mrs de Cortanze and had several children (film-maker Christian de Cortanze; André de Cortanze and his Turbo 16 205, then the Le Mans 905). Then came the war …

Doreen Evans (1916-1982)

Doreen was 17 at the time of her first race at Brooklands in 1933. Her brothers, Dennis and Kenneth, were already racing, and the whole family had spent time at the circuit since it opened in 1907. Moreover, the Evans stable already comprised a Bugatti 35, a Chrysler, a supercharged Zagato Alfa Romeo (ex-Lord Howe from Le Mans), and three six-cylinder MG Magnettes. Mr Evans Senior managed their team, Mrs Evans helped, and their offspring drove. It was in one of these MGs that Doreen made her debut and earned her stripes as a works racing driver. She raced for the MG team at Brooklands and Le Mans in 1935 with Barbara Skinner. She finished in a respectable 25th place. In 1936, her car caught fire at the International Trophy race, and she only just managed to leap from her moving MG, which ended up a charred wreck in the barriers of the paddock. Then all the young set got married. Doreen stopped racing and lived happily with her husband in the United States. She died at home in California at the age of 65.

Doreen Evans and her brother Kenneth at Brooklands. (JFB Collection)

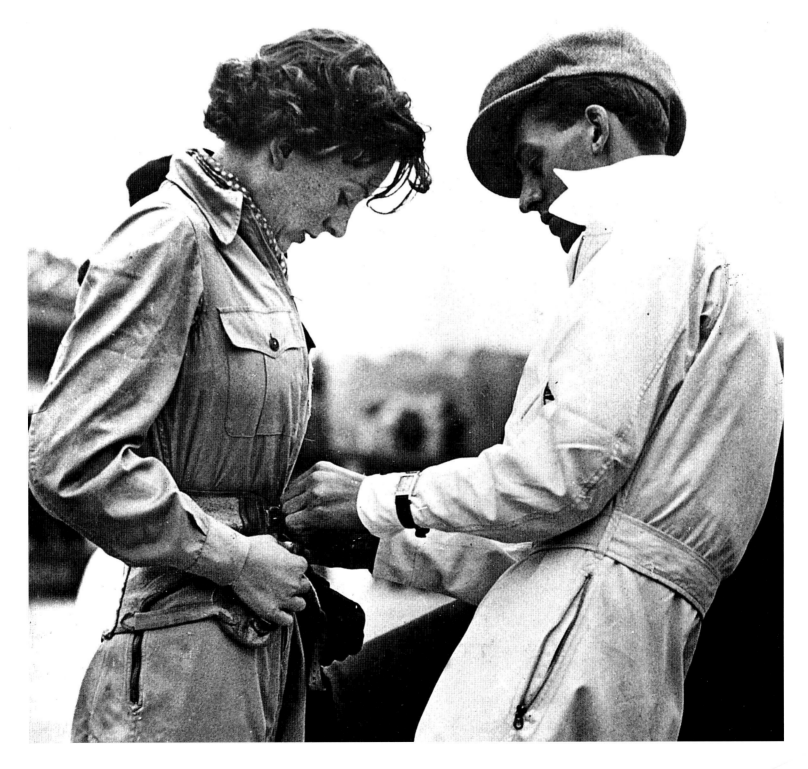

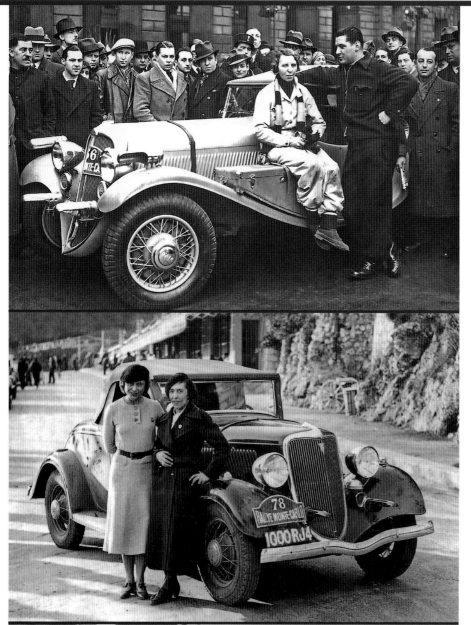

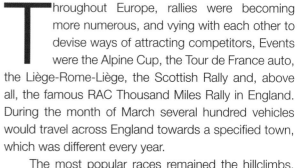

Throughout Europe, rallies were becoming more numerous, and vying with each other to devise ways of attracting competitors, Events were the Alpine Cup, the Tour de France auto, the Liège-Rome-Liège, the Scottish Rally and, above all, the famous RAC Thousand Miles Rally in England. During the month of March several hundred vehicles would travel across England towards a specified town, which was different every year.

The most popular races remained the hillclimbs, such as Shelsley Walsh, and the Brooklands circuit. This was still a time when drivers were all-rounders, and the same champions appeared more or less everywhere. Brooklands was to become a breeding ground for female talent, and 'the girls' – the Brooklands girls – were to become very popular.

Margaret Allen loved horses, but it was in a Lagonda that she began her career. After a visit to Brooklands, she persuaded her father to buy her another, bigger, supercharged Lagonda. Although slight, she always drove very large cars: Bentley 6.5-litres, Frazer Nash, etc. Before getting married in 1937 to Christopher Jennings, Editor of the famous *Motor* magazine, and retiring from racing, she took part in the 1935 Le Mans 24-Hours, with the MG team – a whole band of girls, 'the dancing daughters,' made up of Joan Richmond, Doreen Evans, Mrs Simpson and Barbara Skinner (Skinner's Union, the famous SU carburettors!). She also did several Monte Carlos and an Alpine Cup, which she won. During the war, Margaret Allen was recruited by the Secret Service to work at the highly confidential Bletchley Park, where they were trying to crack the code of the German Enigma machines. Prodigious personalities, the Brits!

Top: Lucy and Laurie Schell at the start of the 1935 Monte Carlo Rally in the Place de la Concorde in their Delahaye 135 Figoni. They finished third overall. (Bavouzet Collection)

Middle: Misses Lamberjack and Marinovitch with their Ford V8. Starting from Palermo, they won the 1935 Ladies' Cup. (Bavouzet Collection)

Misses Darre-Brandt and Christiansen with their large 3-litre Chrysler-Plymouth were fourth of the ladies in the 1934 Monte Carlo. (JFB Collection)

Miss Hustinx and Mrs Leblanc at the Place de la Concorde control with their Peugeot 601, arriving from Stavanger. The radiator thermometer is sited in the middle of the bonnet! (Bavouzet Collection)

XVME RALLYE AUTOMOBILE
MONTE-CARLO

En raison du décès de S. M. le ROI GEORGE V, le Dîner de Gala qui devait être donné le Dimanche 2 Février en l'honneur des Concurrents du XVme Rallye Automobile de Monte-Carlo est supprimé.

La Distribution des Prix primitivement fixée au Dimanche 2 Février à 11 h. aura lieu le même jour à 14 h. 45.

En conséquence, les Concurrents sont priés de se conformer à l'horaire suivant :

A 13 h. 45 : Rassemblement des voitures sur le Quai de Plaisance.
A 14 h. 15 : Défilé.
A 14 h. 45 : Distribution des Prix sur la Place du Palais.

Gala card. The gala at the end of the rally was cancelled due to the death of King George V on 20 January 1936. (JFB Collection)

Mrs Mareuse and Miss Hustinx were 34th to the finish in the rain of the 1936 Monte Carlo, ahead of Des Forest, who was 44th. It was a miserable Monte Carlo right to the end: a year of economic crisis and King George V had just died. There was no gala dinner. (JFB Collection)

The Hillman of Mrs Cotton and Mrs Parnell at the start and finish of the 1937 Monte Carlo. (JFB Collection)

Top left: Mrs Madeleine Rouault and Mrs Suzanne Largeot at the finish of the Monte Carlo on 29 January 1938. They were the first of the ladies. (JFB Collection)

Above and left: The same pair, the following day, at the official prize-giving. Feminity wins the day over being a racing driver; they got out their hats and were glad to see the sun again. (JFB Collection)

Mrs Simon, grinning broadly at having reached the finish, and being second of the ladies in the 1938 Monte Carlo with her Hotchkiss and its chained tyres. (JFB Collection)

Far right: Suzanne Largeot again, but with Mrs Simon in a Hotchkiss at the 1938 Liège-Rome-Liège. Freshly lipsticked, they carried off the Ladies' Cup, despite retiring at Bolzano, the only ladies in the race! (JFB Collection)

The weather wasn't exactly hot in England for the 1932 Thousand Miles Rally. Mrs Benjamin and Mrs Shilitoe fill up with hot water before the start. Others, like Mrs Johnston, touched up their make-up. (JFB Collection)

Bottom of previous page: Finish of the RAC Thousand Miles Rally at Eastbourne in 1935. The finish is in a different town each year. (JB Collection)

Left: But where on earth is Eastbourne? Mrs Jackie Astbury and Cynthia Mason in a Singer in front of The Ace of Spades Garage in Hounslow, during the 1935 RAC Rally. (JFB Collection)

Far left: Everyone was looking for the way to the finish at Eastbourne in 1935. (JFB Collection)

In weak sunshine Mrs Sherer and Mrs Dobson, dressed for battle, push their MG to the start of the Thousand Miles at the Ace of Spades, by the Kingston crossroads, on 24 March 1936. (JFB Collection)

Kitty Brunnel at the Scottish Rally in an MG, leaving London, in 1932. (JFB Collection)

Rallying at Winchcombe in the Cotswolds is no joke. Mrs Goodban and her Singer have no time to pose for photographs. 24 February 1934. (JFB Collection)

A shot of Brooklands in 1932, showing its famous banking. (JFB Collection)

Start of the 2x12-hour relay race, in which several female racing drivers took part. Racing had to stop at night because of the noise and the neighbours. (JFB Collection)

A group of women racing drivers at Brooklands for the Duchess of York Race in 1932. From left to right: Eileen Ellison, Joan Richmond, Mrs Van Dykes, (unknown), Mrs D Burnett, Victoria Worsley, Kay Petre, and Bill Wisdom. (JFB Collection)

Caricatures of women racing drivers at Brooklands in the 1930s, by Bryan de Grineau. (DR)

Fay Taylour, Lady 'Leadfoot'
(1904-1983)

The scandalous Fay Taylour was a real firebrand. A beautiful redhead, well-born, from an aristocratic Irish family from Dublin, she also had the gift of the gab and a corrosive sense of humour. Very athletic, she won £50 in a tennis tournament in 1922 and immediately bought her first car (just like Annie Soisbault thirty years later). In fact, she had known how to drive since the age of twelve.

Mad about speed and racing, she started out on motorbikes on cinder tracks, followed by oval speed tracks. She became famous in England and Australia, where she spent a season. She began her career on four wheels at Brooklands in 1931, at the wheel of a Talbot 105, averaging more than 150km/h (93mph).

The following year, she was again placed second at Brooklands with a Monza Alfa Romeo. After crossing the finish line, she was so excited that she did several laps at top speed, each time almost crashing into the officials, who were not in the least impressed. As a result, she was disqualified and fined. She always raced in a skirt and jacket, and her love of racing was such that she always said that the day she met a man who was harder to handle than a racing car, she would give up racing!

She remained unmarried, claiming that she got her kicks from racing. Like most racing drivers, she had few

Fay Taylour always drove in a skirt and jacket, head band and hardened leather helmet. Brooklands (1933). (Getty Images)

Fay Taylour began her motorbiking career on a dirt track. (JFB Collection)

possessions, and always travelled to the circuits with a suitcase containing only a pair of satin pyjamas. In fact, she had once been taken to hospital after a racing accident, and found herself confronting the press dressed in a hideous straitjacket!

She took part in races the world over, in New Zealand, Miami and Australia. Her finest racing success was a victory in a Triumph Adler, on home ground in Ireland, at the Leinster Trophy road race. She also raced an Aston Martin in the Mille Miglia, and in the 1938 South Africa Grand Prix in Freddy Dixon's Riley. He had his licence revoked for 'having words' with the local police.

Why 'scandalous'? Well, in June 1940, shortly before the conflict reached its height, she was thrown into prison for her pro-Nazi leanings (which perhaps explains the odd choice of a Triumph Adler when racing). She was, in fact, the mistress of Oswald Mosley, the well-known British Fascist leader who had married one of the Mitford sisters. This cost her three years in Holloway prison, along with all the other sympathizers of the Black Shirt movement. A cache of photos of Adolf Hitler was even found in her cell!

After the war, she was one of the few female racing drivers to resume an international career. She returned to Ireland in 1944 and, three years later, was selling agricultural machinery in Dublin. In 1949, the lure of the race track, and a new encounter with a Jaguar dealer from Hollywood put her back on course to Midget car racing on dirt tracks. She then returned to Ireland, even taking part in a few Racer-500 events against young racing drivers like Stirling Moss and Peter Collins. She finally retired to Dorset, where she suffered a heart attack at the age of 80.

Fay Taylour in her supercharged Alfa Romeo Zagato during training. Given the amount of wear on the tyres, it's obvious that money wasn't wasted during the trials! (JFB Collection)

June 1940, Fay Taylour doesn't seem to be concerned by her detention in Holloway Prison. Maybe she doesn't yet know that she is about to spend three years there ... (Getty Images)

Kay Petre (1903-1994)

This darling of the public was a ravishing, slender, doll-like little brunette, always dressed to the nines in her immaculate pale blue racing suit.

When lawyer and pilot Henry Petre (pronounced 'Peter') crossed the threshold of the Brooklands flying club with this beautiful little brunette on his arm, nobody could believe their eyes! Petre, the confirmed bachelor, had got married! He had met her in Canada during a business trip. Kay, the daughter of a wealthy Toronto family, was very athletic and an ice-skating champion. So nobody was surprised when, immersed one day in the atmosphere of the paddocks at Brooklands, she asked her dear husband for racing lessons in his favourite Invicta. She soon showed an aptitude, and he gave her a splendid all-red Wolsley Hornet Daytona Special. She made the podium for her first two women's races, but her racing career only really took off in 1933 when she received her first Bugatti 35C, which she had repainted blue to match her outfits.

She gained a good deal of experience in this Bugatti. In fact, it was during the famous Ladies' Mountain Handicap in October 1933 – at which all the best women racing drivers were present – that the brother of Rita Don, one of Kay's chief rivals, made a bet that his Riley 9, with his sister at the wheel, would be faster than Kay and her Bugatti. We must not forget that these ladies were often accompanied during Brooklands races, so Freddie Dixon took his place next to his sister, who had a bad habit of braking too early before bends. He took a pin and a piece of string, which he attached to the accelerator. During the race, every time Rita lifted her foot to brake, she received a nasty prick and, to an outsider, the Riley appeared to be bounding forward! Although Kay drove with her foot to the floor, the Riley 9, with its faster top speed, won by a short lead of 5.2 seconds. Freddie Dixon won his bet, but had a serious row with his sister after the race!

Although Kay Petre won many solo races, she also began to race in teams, and took part in the pitched battle that existed between the Singer, Austin and MG marques. This selection was to lead them to race at the Le Mans 24-Hours. Kay's partners at Singer were Eileen Ellison and Mrs Tolhurst. The opponents for MG: Margaret Allen, Doreen Evans and Irene Schwelder. In driving rain, Kay finished brilliantly in fifth place and the team qualified for the Wakefield Cup. Kay took part in the 1934 Le Mans with Dorothy Champney in a Riley Ulster (Dorothy was shortly to marry Victor Riley). They finished 13th, and the first of the ladies. Frenchwoman Anne Itier was 17th in an MG.

Kay was a small, slightly-built woman, so, for team races, where she had to take over the wheel from the preceding driver, she had a bucket-cushion system

Kay Petre and Dorothy Champney at Le Mans in 1934, sitting on their feisty little Riley Ulster IMP. They finished 13th overall, happy and dirty! (JFB Collection)

Rita Don and her Riley
9 at Brooklands in 1933.
(JFB Collection)

Rita Don and her brother
racing in her Riley, 13
October 1933. Rita is
being pricked by a pin
held by her brother to
make her accelerate!
Freddie had bet on
beating Kay Petre and
her Bugatti at any price,
which is what happened.
(Nicolosi Collection)

officials began to fear that this would end badly, as both girls had set their hearts on winning. After consultation, they were each granted three last laps of the circuit; the fastest would win the title.

Kay's Delage reached 134.34mph (216.2km/h). Gwenda launched herself but managed only one and a half laps before her silencer exploded, completely smoking her out. Kay Petre won. The next day, a cantankerous Gwenda started again and achieved – though too late – 135.95mph (218.79km/h)! From then on, both girls sported the famous 130mph badge.

Kay again raced a Riley, with Elsie 'Bill' Wisdom, at Le Mans in 1935, then an ERA, and another Riley in the South Africa Grand Prix, where she was also able to test the famous Auto Union V16. She made a successful contribution to the Austin team, on several occasions getting copiously scalded by oil and water from its motors. Her racing career nearly came to a tragic end in 1937, at a time when she was receiving more media coverage than any other female racing driver. Driving a supercharged, single-seater MG in the 500-Mile Race at Brooklands, she was rammed at full speed by Reg Parnell's massive MG. The MG rolled over several times on the track, and Kay spent a year recovering, undergoing several plastic surgery operations. Parnell lost his licence for a year. Kay and Parnell remained good friends despite this, and she was philosophical: "When you practice a dangerous sport like racing, you always risk paying the price one day."

After her recovery, she never regained the same efficiency on circuits, and turned more to rallying, taking part in the Alpine Cup and the Monte Carlo (with Joan Richmond). After the war, she became a journalist, and it was while covering the Monte Carlo that she came even closer to losing her life when her car smashed violently into a lorry at a crossroads near Digne. She escaped by the skin of her teeth.

Kay later became the colour consultant for Austin coachwork, so it's perhaps to her – and her love of pale blue outfits from her time with Bugattis – that we owe the delightful light blue colour found on the Austin Mini 850. Kay passed away peacefully in her London apartment at the age of 91.

Kay Petre and 'Bill'
Wisdom deep in
conversation at
Brooklands before
the 500-mile race on
19 September 1936.
(JFB Collection)

specially made for her, which she installed in the cockpit so that she could reach the pedals!

The high point of the year was her duel with Gwenda Stewart-Hawkes, for the title of fastest lady at Brooklands. Gwenda arrived from Montlhéry in her imposing Derby-Miller 1600, fitted with a special silencer for Brooklands, and Kay chose to borrow Oliver Bertram's old but famous – and enormous – 1924 10.7-litre Delage with which she had already crossed the 129mph (207.6km/h) barrier. Gwenda opened with a lap of 130mph; Kay replied with 134.75mph! The

Kay Petre (with a delightful little bow in her hair) at the start of Le Mans in 1937 in an Austin Seven Grasshopper. She drove with George Mangan, and they had to abandon the race due to a drop in oil pressure in the 72nd lap. No fewer than eight women attended that year: Mrs Itier with Huschke von Hanstein in an Adler, Mrs Simon in a Fiat-Gordini, No 59 in the photo, Miss Eccles, Suzanne Largeot, Miss Ridell, Dorothy Stanley-Turner and Joan Richmond. (JFB Collection)

Kay at the wheel of her Austin, No 3, at the start of the heats for the September 1937 500-mile race, moments away from being rammed and seriously injured by Reg Parnell's big MG. (JFB Collection)

Kay Petre, a member of the Austin works team, at the wheel of her supercharged single-seater. Kay was a favourite with the public, and therefore one of the most popular with the media. (JFB Collection)

23 March 1933 marks the return of Kay Petre to the wheel of her supercharged Riley, six months after her accident. She is still wearing a sticking plaster. This was to be her last race at Brooklands as the enthusiasm was no longer there. After that, she concentrated on rallies, to the great relief of her husband. (JFB Collection)

Eileen Ellison (1910-1967)

One of Kay's partners at Singer in the Wakefield Cup had been the blonde Eileen Ellison. This girl is a mystery as very little is known about her.

Born at Great Shelford, she was mad about racing, thanks to her brother. Not being very wealthy, she raced with a second-hand white Bugatti 37. Her racing career really took off in 1932 when she won the Duchess of York Ladies' Cup against Elsie 'Bill' Wisdom and her Invicta, Fay Taylour in a Talbot, and Kay Petre in her red Hornet.

When she went racing on the continent, Eileen usually towed her 37 behind another road-going Bugatti, and took camping equipment so she could sleep in the circuit paddocks. She achieved respectable positions in hillclimb races, more-or-less throughout Europe: in the Grossglockner; 3rd in the Klausen in rain; at the 1935 Lorraine Grand Prix; 11th in the 1935 Albi Grand Prix (she was lying fourth when her fuel inlet pipe broke). The same thing happened to her at the South Africa Grand Prix in 1936. After getting married in 1940 to squadron leader Brian Lane, who was lost in action in 1942, she went to live permanently in South Africa, where she married Owen Fargus, a wealthy landowner. People say that she was in the habit of swimming in the shark-infested Indian Ocean and that she wasn't afraid, explaining that sharks only eat men! After a comfortable life, they both ended their days in Jersey in the 1960s.

Eileen Ellison at the Albi Grand Prix in 1935 with her Bugatti 37, No 14. She finished seventh after having driven the entire race in fourth position. (Bavouzet Collection)

The blonde Eileen Ellison and her trusty white Bugatti. She won this Duchess of York race at Brooklands in 1932. (DR)

Elsie 'Bill' Wisdom (1904-1972)

Whilst Kay Petre always sported a pale outfit, Elsie Wisdom deliberately chose black, because it showed the dirt less and, perhaps, to also go with her black hair and green eyes. And whilst many women devoted themselves more to racing than to their families, Elsie had married a racing driver, and practised this discipline en famille (like Jill and Bummer Scott). She often brought her little girl, Anne (who went on to become a rally team-mate to the famous Pat Moss, and married Peter Riley), to the paddock. Elsie's six big brothers soon nicknamed her 'Bill,' as she was a real tomboy. She rode her own motorbike at the age of sixteen. Worried about her escapades on two wheels, her parents, as a safety precaution, gave her a small GWK cyclecar, which was soon swapped for a supercharged Lea-Francis and a Frazer-Nash. Tommy Wisdom, her future husband, was a brilliant young journalist for a motorsports magazine.

Bill and Tom Wisdom (Brooklands, 1933). (JFB Collection)

Elsie 'Bill' Wisdom in trials at the wheel of her Frazer-Nash at Brooklands, on 21 March 1930, for the opening of the season. (JFB Collection)

September 1932. Bill Wisdom at the wheel of the Thomas-Special, which sparked a media frenzy. The Brooklands officials, who doubted her ability to control this monster, obliged her to take a driving test before the race. (JFB Collection)

When he met Bill, he fell helplessly and instantly in love with this girl who raced a Frazer-Nash with chain transmission!

No sooner had Tommy married Bill, he entered her in a race at Brooklands (without consulting her!) and she did extremely well to win. She also beat Tom in the hillclimb race at Shelsley Walsh. From then on, Tom often had to admit that his wife was faster than him. In 1932, Tom bought her Lord Howe's enormous Leyland-Thomas. Ever wary of women, the Brooklands officials banned her from taking part in the Three Laps Ladies Handicap Race, obliging her to take a racing test in front of a panel of officials before acknowledging her fitness to drive the enormous 7.2-litre car! She also won the race and her famous 120mph (193km/h) badge.

She shared the driving with her husband; this gave her, she said "endless topics of conversation" ... She raced with the Australian Joan Richmond in a Riley 9, in the 2x12-hour relay and the 1932 Thousand Miles. This was a total success, and they won the race ahead of all the male racers and the best European works teams.

Bill entered the Le Mans several times, including in 1933, with Mortimer Goodall in an Austin-Martin. During the night, her engine exploded and she had to walk home. On the way, she came across a first-aid post, and was asked what she was doing there. With what little French she possessed, she replied: "Voiture Bang!" Everyone believed her to be the victim of an accident, and a doctor dragged her into a tent for the requisite medical check. She struggled fiercely, having heard about the 'lecherous' French men, and ran off!

In 1935, Tom was in a Singer and Bill in a Riley with Kay Petre. They both deserted during the night, and Tom found his wife at the Riley team's hotel. The next morning, on taking the breakfast tray up to Bill's room, the chambermaid gave them a very knowing look on discovering a strange man between the sheets ... She found it hard to believe that this was Bill's husband.

In 1937, the Wisdom family was taking part in the Thousand Miles in an MG, but smashed into a tree to avoid a pedestrian, sustaining a broken leg for Tom and crushed face for Bill – a bad year. They were also to take part in Alpine Cups and the Monte Carlo.

War broke out and, as with many men and women racing drivers, the years of conflict put an end to their careers. Brooklands closed. The mood was no longer conducive to women on the tracks: public-spiritedness required that every woman look after her war veteran husband and produce children. Serious accidents sustained by Hellé Nice in 1936 and Kay Petre in 1937 meant that interest in watching women risking their lives on the racecourse waned. This was a time for discretion and patriotism, which was why a good many of them opted to race more discreetly in rallies. A new generation of racing drivers was on the horizon.

Bill was to take part in several Monte Carlo rallies between 1949 and 1951. She and her husband again took part in the 1951 Alpine Cup, which almost killed them. A tourist with a huge American car, travelling in the opposite direction to the rally, accidentally smashed into their Bristol. The hand of destiny? It was time to make way for the younger Ann 'Wizz' Wisdom, with her colleague Pat Moss, who would claim victory after victory in their beautiful Austin-Healey.

Top: Bill Wisdom and Joan Richmond preparing themselves at the wheel of their Riley 9, for the Brooklands 2x12-Hours in June 1932. (JFB Collection)

Above: Bill Wisdom and Kay Petre at the 1935 Le Mans in a Riley MPH. It was abandoned at lap 38 with engine failure. (JFB Collection)

Anne-Cécile Itier (1895-?)

Anne-Cécile Itier had married a Mr Rose, a Scotsman, who used to beat her. A pretty, petite but determined redhead, she divorced him. Having always been attracted by speed, she began by trying her hand at flying, then moved to motorcars at the age of thirty-one. "She devoted herself to competition in a spirit of liberty and independence." This was in 1926 when suffragettes and bobbed hair were in their heyday.

Anne-Cécile began with an amateur rally, which she finished, in a Brasier. After three years of secondary races, she felt ready to enter a Grand Prix for small cars, doing so in Bordeaux in a 500cc Sima-Violet, which she won. In 1929, her career was launched. From then on she drove a Bugatti. Over the next seven years she competed against the best racing drivers: Raymond Sommer, Robert Benoist, Pierre Veyron, and Hellé Nice, from the La Baule Grand Prix to those of Comminges, Nîmes, Tunisie, Berne, Nürburgring … She also competed five times at Le Mans between 1930 and 1939.

In fact, it was at the 1937 Le Mans that she raced a revolutionary ultra-streamlined German Adler Triumf saloon for the Adler works team, sharing the driving with the dashing Baron von Hanstein. A month earlier, at the Morocco rally, she had raced a cabriolet for the Hanomag team with Mrs Mareuse. They were both unaware that this German team was there to also carry out an intelligence mission for the Abwehr, which was trying to analyse the French military forces in Morocco. What a fine cover these two pretty little Frenchwomen were, though they were caught in a stifling sandstorm and then a terrible blizzard in the Atlas Mountains. They owed their lives entirely to the same Huschke von Hanstein and his Hanomag, who stopped and took on board a quite frozen and almost hysterical Anne-Cécile. His team-mate got in beside Mrs Mareuse, of course, and this incident allegedly led to a fine romance after he warmed her up … Finally, within sight of the rally checkpoint, everyone took their proper places, and the officials didn't suspect a thing! The legend of the handsome spy who came in from the cold was to live on.

Anne-Cécile appeared again at the 1938 Paris Grand Prix, where she finished third with Germaine Rouault in a Delahaye, and in 1939 in a Hanomag-Diesel for the last Monte Carlo before the war. But Anne-Cécile was not to fall, as Violette Morris did, under the influence of Nazi propaganda. Perhaps because our racing baron, the seductive Huschke von Hanstein, was not convinced by the regime either (he was arrested by the Gestapo in 1943 and sent to the Russian Front).

Before this period of hostilities that was to suspend life in the racing world, Anne-Cécile, along with the 'Bugattiste' Jean Delorme, developed the Union Sportive Automobile (USA), and organized races. We are particularly indebted to her for the women's races at Grand Prix openings with Juvaquatre cars (Hellé Nice), but war broke out, and Anne-Cécile founded a unit of military couriers. Right up untill the armistice, they bravely carried letters under fire from machine guns, and saved refugees. She went on to compete in a few Monte Carlo rallies in Renault 4CV, then spent her days quietly on the Cote d'Azur in the 1960s. Maybe she even met Hellé Nice towards the end of her sad life; after all, they had the seductive Baron von Hanstein in common …

Opposite page: Anne Itier with her Bugatti T51 at the 1934 Berne Grand Prix during preparation before the start. She was to finish in a gutsy ninth place. This Bugatti was wrecked a year later, during the Picardy Grand Prix, due to an error on the part of the mechanic. (Cimarosti Collection)

Anne-Cécile Itier and her Simca Fiat at Crystal Palace in June 1938. (Bavouzet Collection)

Mrs Eccles at Brooklands in 1936. She drove an Eccles Rapier special. (JFB Collection)

Mrs Eccles and her supercharged Rapier in 1936. (JFB Collection)

In the end there were a good many of them, these 'Brooklands girls.' The male racing drivers had good reason to be wary of them, as they clinched more than just places of honour. Marjorie, the wife of Roy Eccles, swept the board of the banked tracks, but also those at Crystal Palace in 1936 (where she did a spectacular roll in her supercharged Rapier), and Le Mans 24-Hours races with Freddy Clifford. They retired in lap 125 with magneto failure, leaving the way clear for Suzanne Largeot, Dorothy Stanley-Turner, Joan Riddell and Joan Richmond, who all came within the first 20 places.

Nor was Dorothy Paget a weakling in her lumbar support belt at the wheel of her Bentley Blower. The younger women, like Dorothy Stanley-Turner and Yvonne Maure, were just as promising in the hillclimb races of 1938 and 1939, but the war also intervened for them.

There weren't only English women at Le Mans; since 1930, a generation of women racing drivers made their mark there, and these were pretty Frenchwomen, Odette Siko and Marguerite Mareuse (Christian de Cortanze's mother-in-law – it's a small world!), who opened fire with a gallant seventh position overall in the only Bugatti present that summer of 1930. Mrs Mareuse was very sporty, and it was a bad fall that took her away from horse riding and led her to discover and compete in motor racing. This was also a one-two for Bentley, thanks to Mrs Dorothy Paget's stable with the famous Woolf Barnato and Gled Kidstone, who won.

Odette Siko was to compete each year until 1933. Up to ten women raced in 1935.

Marjorie Eccles and Freddy Clifford about to take the start for Le Mans in 1937 in their Singer. (JFB Collection)

Above, left: Dorothy Stanley-Turner and her MG at Brooklands, on 11 March 1938. (JFB Collection)

Marguerite Mareuse and Odette Siko in a Bugatti 40 finished seventh overall at the 1930 Le Mans. They were the first women to race at Le Mans. (JFB Collection)

Marjorie Eccles and her Singer, No 50, Le Mans. She was to retire in the 125th lap with ignition problems. (JFB Collection)

4

The Second World War had come and gone and nothing would ever be the same again: attitudes had changed and reconstruction was the order of the day. In France, cars were rationed, and considerable imagination was required in order to obtain one of the new Renault 4CVs (known as the little 'block of butter,' owing to the creamy yellow colour of the Afrikacorps surplus), or the placid Peugeot 203s from Sochaux. Resort to foreign production for a Jaguar XK 120 or the fledgling Ferraris? Perish the thought! (The Porsche 356, like all German cars, was viewed with suspicion … It was 1953, and Porsche importer Auguste Veuillet was having a hard job selling it.)

The rally
years
1950

Rolls-Royce Silver Cloud, picnic table and Formica. London Motor Show, 1955. (JFB Collection)

The Contessa delle Chiesa in the 1952 Paris-Saint-Raphaël. Animals were allowed, but had to be weighed! (Bavouzet Collection)

No longer was anyone amazed by women racing behind the wheel of enormous machines as they had achieved even greater things throughout the war. In France and England, large-scale press campaigns exhorted public spiritedness and required women to spend more time looking after their husbands returning from the war, and to have children. The circuits had been occupied by billeted regiments, and Spa, Montlhéry, Le Mans and Brooklands were licking their wounds. At Le Mans, the grandstands had been dismantled by the occupying troops, almost down to the last screw, and taken away – nobody knows where. There was just one skeleton of a stand and the Michelin start and finish posts on the 13km (8 mile) track!

All the women who raced before the war were now ten years older. Mrs Betty Haig, Anna Maria Peduzzi (the 'Moroccan girl'), Yvonne Simon, Germaine Rouault, Charlotte Versigny, Fernande Hustinx (who had since become Mrs de Cortanze), Greta Molander (still with her Saab and little pointed hat), amongst others, had their work cut out against the young up-and-coming class. These youngsters, like Gilberte Thirion and Annie Bousquet, began to obtain results at rallies and at Le Mans. Older newcomers, such as Marie Honoré, Ginette Sigrand, Lise Renaud or Régine Gordine, battled it out and monopolized the places of honour in rallies.

Because rallies are more low-key and more politically correct for women, it's there that we find them, spread between Monte Carlo, the Mille Miglia, the Alpine Cup and the Paris-Saint-Raphaël.

Marie Honoré

The war had forced Marie Honoré to begin rallying late in life, but she was still a fine figure of a woman and wielded the steering wheel with a flourish. To compensate for all the years lost during occupation, she doubled her participation in all of the big French rallies – Monte Carlo, Paris-Saint-Raphaël, the Alpine Cup and Charbonnières, with her trusty four-door Alfa Romeo TI that she shared with Suzanne Donckele and Renée Wagner – and spent the rest of her time running her business of transporting fruit and vegetables in Lille. She then moved to a Giulietta coupé with Anne-Marie Spiers, and a Jaguar MkII.

Marie Honoré was also mother to the famous Lille racing driver Robert Dutoit (who always came second). They only ever teamed up once and ended up in the parapet of a bridge in the 1958 Routes du Nord. Henceforth, Marie was to accompany her son on his races, providing support. At the Tour de France auto, she even transported a folding bed to him between stages!

Racing starts up again. The programme of the 1947 female Paris Rally. (JFB Collection)

Mrs Deutch and Mrs Bonnet in the DB owned by their respective husbands in the 1948 GP d'élégance, Bois de Boulogne. (Nicolosi Collection)

Décidément imbattable
La 4 CV triomphe partout

Le même jour, la 4 CV Renault remporte
LA Iʳᵉ PLACE AU CLASSEMENT GÉNÉRAL TOUTES CATÉGORIES
dans 2 épreuves totalement différentes :

Rallye International des
ROUTES du NORD

Rallye Féminin
PARIS · Sᵗ RAPHAËL

1ᵉʳ GUY LAPCHIN
et Madame LAPCHIN
712 Km
(moyenne imposée de 60 km/h avec contrôles secrets)

1ʳᵉ Madame SIMON
3ᵉ Madame POCHON - 4ᵉ Madame DELORME
1.500 Km en 4 étapes
(Aix-en-Provence - Sestrières - San-Remo - Saint-Raphaël)

CE N'EST PAS PAR HASARD
que la 4 CV gagne le même jour sur les plus mauvaises
routes pavées du Nord et dans les cols des Alpes.

CE N'EST PAS PAR HASARD
que la 4 CV gagne le même jour les deux épreuves
de classement : vitesse en côte et difficile épreuve
d'accélération-maniabilité.

CE N'EST PAS PAR HASARD
que la 4 CV gagne le même jour, l'une entre les mains
d'un architecte, excellent conducteur, l'autre pilotée
par une jolie femme, remarquable conductrice.

CE N'EST PAS PAR HASARD
qu'à la première place figure...

encore et toujours... une 4 CV

*Renault propaganda.
(JFB Collection)*

*Marie Honoré transported
fruit and vegetables during
the week, and raced cars at
weekends. (JFB Collection)*

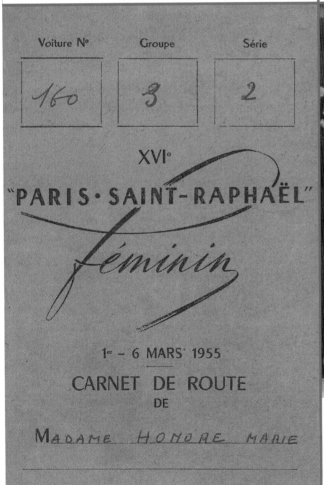

Voiture Nº	Groupe	Série
160	3	2

XVIᵉ
"PARIS · SAINT-RAPHAËL"
féminin

1ᵉʳ – 6 MARS 1955

CARNET DE ROUTE
DE

MADAME HONORE MARIE

*The time-card book for
No 160. (JFB Collection)*

*Marie Honoré and Suzanne Donckele in their
Alfa TI in the XVIe Paris-Saint-Raphaël, in
March 1954. The team had to pull out of the
race between Gap and Montgenèvre because
the car broke down. (JFB Collection)*

Marie Honoré and Renée Wagner at the Charbonnières with the Alfa TI. (JFB Collection)

Marie Honoré and Mrs Etalet, at the 1956 Rallye des Alpes. (JFB Collection)

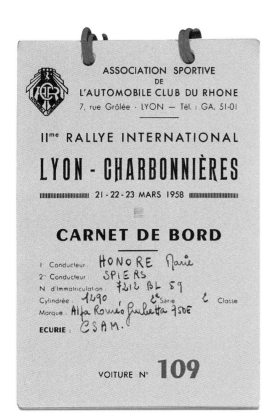

Régine Gordine, Princess of Bashkir and Kantismansis (1915-)

Régine Bruno was very young when she married a monsieur Peter, a scrap-metal wholesaler. She was already passionate about motorcars, had taken part in rallies before the war with Germaine Rouault, and drove around every day in a Delahaye 135 MS Figoni cabriolet. She was very friendly with Suzanne Largeot, the owner of a driving school, and Mrs Versigny, who had raced at Le Mans and done several Monte Carlo rallies. Régine was recruited by Germaine Rouault to make up the Le Mans team in 1950, in a Simca-Gordini roadster. That year, along with Yvonne Simon and Betty Haig in a Ferrari, they were the last women to participate in this trial for a long time. She also did a Monte Carlo in 1952 with Mrs Simon in a Simca sport.

Slim and pretty at 1.57m (5ft 1½in) and 47kg (7½st), Régine Peter was selling second-hand locomotives in the George V bar when film producer Sacha Gordine walked into the room. It was love at first sight for both of them, and she soon became Mrs Sacha Gordine.

Sacha was very exuberant and life was one long round of partying and fun. The Gordines mixed with numerous actors and actresses – Gabin, Pagnol, Martine Carol, Simone Signoret, and Marcel Carné – but also with the racing fraternity: Olivier Gendebien, Maurice Trintignant, the young Jean Rédélé, Georges Houel and Annie Soisbault. Between making films that enjoyed varying degrees of success (he produced *Orfeu Negro* by Marcel Camus, *Dédé d'Anvers*, and *Bari chien*

Régine Gordine visiting the Salon de l'Auto in Paris in 1954. A beautiful, stylish lady, she was part of Parisian high society. (Blanchet Collection)

Régine Gordine and Mrs Boeswillwald at the 1951 Tour de France auto. They finished 50th overall with their 203. (Blanchet Collection)

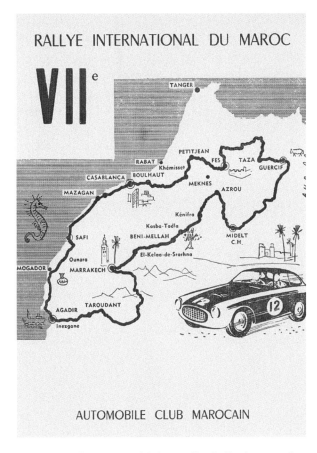

RALLYE INTERNATIONAL DU MAROC

VIIe

AUTOMOBILE CLUB MAROCAIN

Gordine and Terray at the 1954 Monte Carlo, 36th overall, but still smiling. (Blanchet Collection)

Far left: 1953 Moroccan Rally programme. (Blanchet Collection)

Below left: Régine Gordine and Irène Terray at the 1953 Liège-Rome-Liège in a Coupé 203 special from the Écureuils stable. (Blanchet Collection)

The same pair, clocking in at Gênes. (JFB Collection)

Régine was unaware she was pregnant during the 1955 Monte Carlo, consequently the first rally for little Sacha Gordine junior (the name Sacha was passed down from father to son in this old aristocratic Russian family, the Gregorieffs, princess of Bashkir and Kantismansis.) Then there was the Charbonnières in 1955, and many more.

Whilst in the lead during a Tour de France with Germaine Rouault, who had held the women's record at the Turbie trial, Régine handed her the wheel. Germaine slipped up, and they rolled over twice. The jack struck Régine on the head and the car caught fire. The firemen put it out … and off they went again.

Meanwhile, Sacha Gordine was trying to develop his own Grand Prix car, which he intended Jean Behra to use in the Pau Grand Prix. The project was a flop, and the three cars ended up under a tarpaulin on a barge on the river Seine.

While driving her 203 works special (she always liked to drive French cars) during the 1956 Monte Carlo with Irène Terray, Régine had a serious accident in fog, smashing into a badly-lit timber lorry. This put a stop to her racing career, after which she was only to enter a few casual races. Following the death of Sacha Gordine in 1968, she married printer and racing driver Léon Storez, the father of the lamented Claude Storez, who smashed his Porsche Spyder 550 on the Rheims circuit on the Routes du Nord in 1959. Now 92, Régine Gordine-Storez lives quietly in Paris, where her son, Sacha, cares for her.

loup, as well as some third-rate films), Sacha raced at Le Mans and was very friendly with Amédée Gordini. It was, therefore, logical that Régine Gordine should carry on likewise. She raced in the Liège-Rome-Liège in a 203 coupé and at the Critérium des Alpes in 1954.

Pat Lyons (1927-)

Being the daughter of Sir William Lyons, founder of Jaguar Cars, and marrying Ian Appleyard, Jaguar dealer, brilliant tennis player and Olympic skiing champion, was bound to put Pat Lyons' career as a racing driver somewhat in the shade! Pat was, of course, the navigator worthy of repeated successes in the Alpine Cup with NUB 120, the legendary white XK 120 roadster.

Ian and Pat were the most famous motor racing couple at that time. Newly married, they took part, under the guise of a honeymoon, in the Tulip Rally in Holland in their brand new XK. Then they won the Alpine Cup four times in a row, between 1950 and 1953. But Pat Appleyard also took the wheel in other rallies, including the London Rally in 1951 and the Morecambe in 1952, where she achieved excellent results, and won ladies' cups. Sadly, both stopped racing in 1952 when Ian had to go back to managing his business and take over from his father at the Jaguar agency in Leeds.

Pat Appleyard and her husband, Ian, in their famous 1950 Alpine-Cup Jaguar XK 120, NUB 120, happy to be back in London, safe and sound. (Viart Collection)

Pat and Ian Appleyard with the next Jaguar, RUB 120, after victory at the 1953 Alpine Cup. (Viart Collection)

Roberta Cowell (1921-)

In August 1957, in an Emeryson-Alta, Roberta Cowell beat the record by 0.32 seconds held by Patsy Burt's Cooper in the Shelsley Walsh hillclimb race, and, to Patsy's fury, claimed the Ladies' Cup. As if that was not bad enough, in fact, Patsy Burt had been beaten by an actual World War II Spitfire fighter pilot …

Flight Lieutenant Robert Marshall Cowell had been the first English transsexual to undergo a sex change operation and be allowed to legally change sex in 1951. Bob Cowell was not a particularly effeminate character, and there was nothing to indicate this surprising change of personality. Before the war, he had even lived life as a typical British citizen; getting married and having two children. A lover of racing, engineering and aviation, perhaps influenced by the proximity of the aerodrome at Croydon, where he lived, he enlisted in the RAF at the age of 17 to take flying lessons, and obtained his pilot's licence in a Tiger Moth in 1937. The previous year, having barely reached the age of legal requirement, with his driving licence under his belt he raced a Riley in the Land's End Trial and won his class! He then began to hang around the Brooklands circuit. Being a resourceful man, and having no ticket to show the fierce doorman guarding the entrance to the paddock, Bob hit on the idea of borrowing an old set of overalls and a bucket of water … and nonchalantly walked through to spend his day helping the mechanics and racing drivers.

On becoming an engineer, the whole of his meagre salary went towards buying and maintaining racing cars. For him, the year of 1939 was a good racing season. However, on the other side of the Rhine, a certain moustached man was preparing to change the course of his life. War broke out and Robert Cowell's dream of becoming a fighter pilot in those fantastic machines called Spitfires was about to come true: the country needed pilots and, after a few months' training, he was allocated to a squadron in the south of England. He took part in the Normandy landings and in the Battle of France, when he was shot down in action above Austria, to spend the rest of the war in a German prisoner-of-war camp near Lubeck, freed by the Russians in May 1945. On his return to England, everything had changed.

Naturally, Cowell developed a business preparing racing cars, took part in some competitions in Altas and ERAs at the Rouen Grand Prix, and the 1947 Brighton Speed Trial, but did not feel at all happy in himself due to strong surges of female hormones which were beginning to make him feel 'different.' Following a deep depression and some time with a psychiatrist, he decided 'to go the way nature intended for him' and embarked on the long process of becoming Roberta Cowell.

After the final aesthetical operation in 1951 – and having regained her psychological equilibrium – Roberta, the first British transsexual, came out in broad daylight dressed as a woman, her civil status to be legally rectified. Even though, in her autobiography, Roberta claims to have drawn a line beneath her masculine past, her passion for all things mechanical remained as strong as ever (had she not admitted to taking a small flask of Castrol R and racing petrol to sniff during the war as a reminder of her Brooklands dreams?). So keen was she on racing, that she returned several times to the wheel, notably to Shelsley Walsh hillclimb in 1957, and later on, during the 1970s, when she was to test Tony Kitchiner's Formula 3. What staying power, Roberta!

Far left: Bob Cowell at Brooklands in 1939. (DR)

Roberta Cowell (1954). (DR)

Mr and Mrs Lee Kennard in their Mercedes SSK during the Brighton Run of September 1950. (JFB Collection)

Mrs Allard in an Allard at Brighton in September 1947. (JFB Collection)

Madeira Drive, the Brighton seafront. Joan Gerard and her Riley, in September 1947. (JFB Collection)

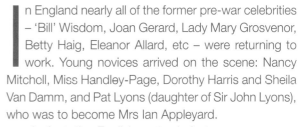

In England nearly all of the former pre-war celebrities – 'Bill' Wisdom, Joan Gerard, Lady Mary Grosvenor, Betty Haig, Eleanor Allard, etc – were returning to work. Young novices arrived on the scene: Nancy Mitchell, Miss Handley-Page, Dorothy Harris and Sheila Van Damm, and Pat Lyons (daughter of Sir John Lyons), who was to become Mrs Ian Appleyard.

In fact, the English motor industry was no more brilliant than the French one, and anything that could be driven was dragged out for racing. The technology deployed for the war effort had not yet filtered through to civilian life. From 1947 to 1949, the pre-war models had a small reprieve and, at the Brighton meeting on Madeira Drive, the famous seafront avenue, the Kennard couple's old SSK, Mrs Allard's Allard, Joan Gerard's Riley and Miss Pilkington's Alfa Zagato 1750 were to be seen dashing past. One had to wait for the 1949 Le Mans before the appearance of a new generation of cars: the brand-new Aston Martin DB2 and the roadsters of Ferrari, a new unknown sporting marque, with its 166 MM. The revolutionary XK 120 arrived in the form of a prototype at the 1948 autumn Paris Salon, but was not really available for another year. It was soon to become famous, thanks to a young English couple called Appleyard.

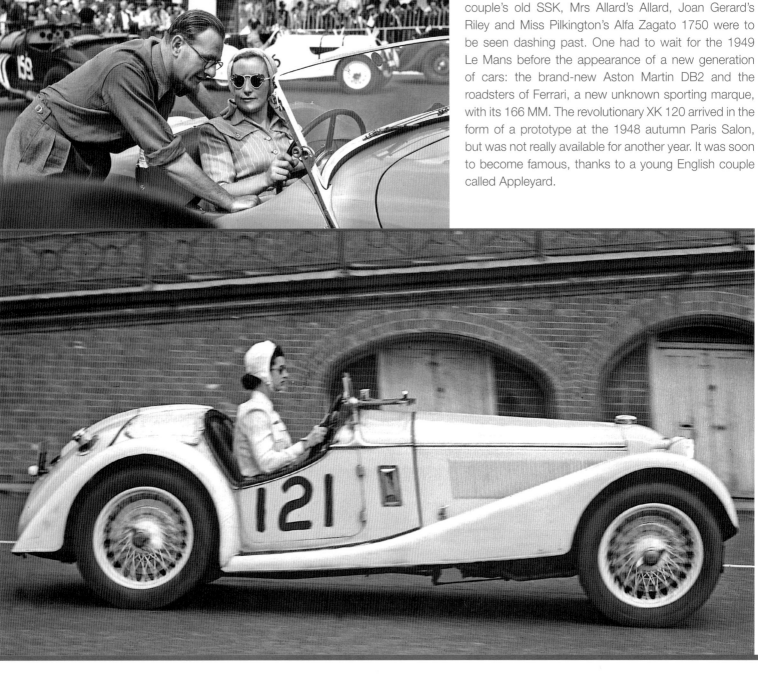

Mrs Pilkington and her Alfa Romeo 1750 at Silverstone, 23 April 1949. (JFB Collection)

Below, left: The women at the 1951 Le Mans: Mrs Simon and Betty Haig in their Ferrari. Yvonne Simon left the road and they were stuck in the sand for a long time. (JFB Collection)

Mrs Simon in the sand; Mrs Rouault filling up her Gordini at Le Mans, 1951. (JFB Collection)

MADAME GERMAINE ROUAULT FAIT LE PLEIN DE SA SIMCA-GORDINI

MADAME SIMON S'EFFORCE DE DESENSABLER SA 'FERRARI'

Bob Cowell in Gosport in his Alta, in 1951. (DR)

Below: Roberta Cowell in Paris in 1952. (DR)

Below, right: Roberta Cowell in the 1970s. (Getty Images)

27ᵉ RALLYE AUTOMOBILE MONTE-CARLO

Mrs Itier (right), back in action at the 1951 Monte Carlo, with Mrs Rispal and a 4CV.

Far left: 1958 Monte Carlo Rally programme. (JFB Collection)

A few years passed by and everyone was determined to forget that dark decade. The automobile clubs were reorganised. In France, the famous 'fonds de course,' a racing fund, was raised to help the French motor industry produce a new generation of high-powered Grand Prix racing cars. The Le Mans 24-Hours restarted in 1949, as did the Monte Carlo rally. We would still have to wait until 1951 for our ladies' special, the Paris-Saint-Raphaël (and the Tour de France auto).

The Countesses Van Limburg-Stirrum and Van Vredenburgh in a Ford V8. First of the ladies and 12ᵗʰ overall in the 1949 Monte Carlo. (JFB Collection)

Greta Molander (1908-2002)

It was on the road to Monte Carlo that our women racing drivers resumed their exploits, more in tuned saloon cars as sports cars appeared only in dribs and drabs. To compete with the hordes of modest Panhards, 4CVs and 203s, as well as with English cars with complicated names and some rare giant American cars (not really in their element in rallies), a few odd beasts like the Saab appeared. The Swedish Greta Molander was neither a novice nor a spring chicken, having already won the Ladies' Cup in the 1937 Monte Carlo in a large Plymouth, and taking part in numerous Nordic rallies after learning to drive her father's car at the age of 16.

Greta had a brief career as a stunt girl in Hollywood and in Midget-car racing in Honolulu. She then spent three months in prison during the war for insulting a German officer! In 1950, with one of the first Saab 92s to come off the production line, she won the Ladies' Cup in the Swedish Rally. Ever faithful to Saab – and always sporting a delightful bobble hat or a little pointed hat – this was the first of a long string of victories in the Tulip Rally, the Midnight Sun Rally, and Sestrières, until 1959. She was to continue driving in historic rallies for a long time, as full of good humour as ever, and cursing behind Sunday drivers who dawdled on her roads!

Greta Molander in the first of her series of Saabs at the 1951 Monte Carlo. She was to remain loyal to this marque for a long time, and win many cups. (JFB Collection)

Far right: Greta Molander again, and one of her delightful little hats. The first of the ladies in 1952, still in a Saab 92. (JFB Collection)

Monte Carlo, 1960. Another Ladies' Cup for Greta Molander and Mrs Lundberg, but this time in a Saab 93. (JFB Collection)

Sheila Van Damm (1922-1987)

One Englishwoman stands out from the rest: Sheila Van Damm, who was European rally champion in 1954 and 1955 with Talbot Sunbeams and the Roots team. Sheila was the daughter of Vivian Van Damm, owner of the Windmill Theatre in London. This theatre became famous for being the first to put on a striptease to raise the morale of British troops, and also for never having closed throughout the painful period of the Blitz.

On finishing her studies at the outbreak of war, Sheila enrolled in the Women's Auxiliary Air Force (WAAF) and served as a military courier. After the war, she acquired her pilot's licence and became an RAF reserve officer.

In 1950, life was returning to normal in London, and, in a bid to create some publicity for their theatre, Mr Van Damm entered his daughter in the *Daily Express* Rally, navigated by Windmill striptease artistes. The Windmill girls' team was a great success, and even came in third. Impressed, the Roots factory invited the team to the 1951 Monte Carlo in a works Hillman Minx – which won the Ladies' Cup. They were on their way! Sheila Van Damm, of the slightly chubby but always smiling face, would have the young Stirling Moss as stablemate. Accompanied by Anne Hall, she won Ladies' Cups here, there and everywhere: at the Tulip Rally, in the Alpine rallies, in the Monte Carlo, and in the Mille Miglia. Although she covered over 14,000 miles (22,530km) in rallies each year, she still found time to look after her theatre during these five years of non-stop racing, engineering the debuts of actors such as Peter Sellers, Tony Hancock, etc. Alongside Betty Hill, she was also the president of the famous Doghouse Club, the WMRAC, where the female colleagues and all the wives (left at home) of the male racing drivers met up. Its emblem was a chequered dog kennel painted in British Racing Green, designed by the famous English humourist, Russell Brockbank.

Towards the end of her life she was to sell the Windmill Theatre, write for *Motor Racing* magazine, and retire with her sister to the countryside, where she looked after a small farm in Sussex. She died in London in August 1987.

Badge of the Dog House Club, founded by Betty Hill and presided over by Sheila Van Damm: a club for the wives of male racing drivers, left at home during the races. (JFB Collection)

Top: Sheila Van Damm at the 1952 Monte Carlo. She didn't win again that year, coming 129th overall. (JFB Collection)

Sheila Van Damm, European female Rally Champion in 1954, seen here in her Sunbeam with Anne Hall and Françoise Clarke after the Monte Carlo. (JFB Collection)

The 1950s were an international breeding ground for women rally drivers. The English liked to finish a Monte Carlo in January on the Côte d'Azur. The Parisian upper crust used to meet up for the Paris-Saint-Raphaël in March. Those who had just completed a Monte Carlo would feel as though they were just getting into their stride, and then it was off for a little Mille Miglia – the Italian 1000 miles – in May, an Alpine Cup in July, a Tour de France auto in September, a Tour de Corse in November, a final Morocco Rally in December, and a prize-giving and gala dinner in the ACF salons. And what a busy season that was!

Now more of them eagerly awaited winning this Ladies' Cup: Nancy Mitchell, the Countess Van Limburg-Stirum, Anne Itier (still around in 1951), Miss Handley-Page, Dorothy Harris, Fernande de Cortanze, the Hammersleys (mother and daughter), Dorothy Stanley-Turner, Madeleine Pochon, Yvonne Terray, Madeleine Blanchoud, etc.

Mrs Grounds and her Jowett Javelin. Monte Carlo 1952. (JFB Collection)

Mrs Stanley-Turner and Mrs Mitchell in Alvis Grey-Lady, Avenue d'Lena, at the start of the 1953 Monte Carlo. They were to come 298th out of 440 ranked competitors. (JFB Collection)

Mrs and Miss Hammersley in a 203 in the 1952 Monte Carlo. (JFB Collection)

Mrs Bizeray in the Bol d'Or at Montlhéry in 1953, in a very special 4CV. She also went on to race in the Nürburgring with the same car. (JFB Collection)

Mrs Blanchoud and Mrs Wagner win the Ladies' Cup in a Giulietta at the 1958 Monte Carlo. (JFB Collection)

Madeleine Pochon and Irène Terray in their little 4CV. They won the 1953 Monte Carlo Ladies' Cup and came 49th overall. (JFB Collection)

Gilberte Thirion (1928-2008)

With a figure like hers, Gilberte could have been a film star, and did, in fact, have a meteoric career. With its Spa Francorchamps circuit (the equivalent of Le Mans) and Liège-Rome-Liège rally, Belgium was another country with a passion for motorsport.

Exhausted by the heat of a fine July afternoon, and, most of all, five hours' of racing, a girl pushed her old broken-down Gordini into the pits before keeling over in a faint. She was third, behind Moss and Chiron, but her distributor had other ideas. This determination to the point of exhaustion was utterly typical of Gilberte Thirion, the daughter of a well-off Belgian industrialist who had won the 1934 Liège-Rome-Liège in a Bugatti.

Gilberte Thirion and Manuel Fangio at the finish of the Rheims Grand Prix in July 1951. (JFB Collection)

He married a fashion model, so it was hardly surprising that Gilberte was a ravishing brunette with a radiant smile that featured in all her photos.

At 19, Gilberte embarked on a secretarial course, and was employed by her father soon afterwards at Champion, a brand of sparkplug that he imported to Belgium. She soon became responsible for public relations and, as she frequented the circuits, often bumped into great racing drivers such as Ascari, Moss, Chiron or Fangio. In 1952, Max Thirion had the chance to buy her a Porsche 356 Gmünd in aluminium. The same year they took part together in their first Paris-Saint-Raphaël, and came second in their category. This was the beginning of an all too short racing career, lasting five years and allowing her to rub shoulders with the greatest.

Gilberte felt comfortable with an engine at the rear, and Porsche became her favourite marque, although she also raced Gordinis, Mercedes, Ferraris … and Renaults.

Gilberte's potential was, of course, soon spotted by Porsche, which perhaps explains why her navigator in Ladies' Cups was often Ingeborg Polenski, whose husband worked for the famous Stuttgart marque, or else Gonzague Olivier (father of Jean-Claude Olivier, director of Yamaha during the Sonauto period). After an initial year in 1952 of learning the ropes, mechanical breakdowns and setbacks (she was unfairly downgraded immediately after winning the Ladies' Cup in the Tour de France automobile), the following years were rather better, and she won other Ladies' Cups, and even the scratch. Racing became her profession, with a punishing schedule at a rate of roughly one rally or race per month. She took part in the Spa Grand Prix, the Paris 24-Hours, the Rheims 12-Hours, Sebring – and even the Le Mans qualifications!

She was a close friend of Annie Bousquet, with whom she often shared her car, and they were to be seen together at the Mille Miglia in a Gordini roadster or at Spa in a small Fiat saloon. In 1954, Gilberte met the

Opposite:

Main picture: Gilberte and Max Thirion, her father, win their class in the Rallye Soleil in 1952. (Mertens Collection)

Right: Gilberte Thirion and Ingelborg Polensky at the 1952 Tour Auto with their Porsche. They were to be unfairly relegated for having received too much support from a banned source: Mrs Polensky's husband, who worked for Porsche. So Madeleine Pochon, in a 4CV, claimed the Ladies' Cup. (JFB Collection)

Gilberte Thirion's Belgian racing licence for a champion. (Mertens Collection)

handsome and distinguished Olivier Gendebien, and, to the delight of the popular press, they became the most handsome racing couple of the 1950s, for they were frequently teamed up in rallies and circuits, in a Porsche, Gordini or Mercedes. But their destiny was never sealed by marriage, and Gilberte set off again with renewed vigour along Europe's roads and racecourses.

In 1956, fate dealt a cruel blow to her entourage. Almost before Gilberte's eyes, Annie Bousquet was killed at the age of 34 when her Spyder 550 overturned in the grass during the Rheims 12-Hours in which they were both racing. Gilberte, in her Gordini, retired immediately and found it hard to get over this event.

To the great delight of Il Commendatore Enzo Ferrari, Gilberte made the Ferrari team twice in 1956 – in a Ferrari 500TR with Anna Maria Peduzzi in the Paris Mille Kilomètres, and at the Supercortemaggiore Grand Prix in Monza – coming 10th overall on each occasion, but what a media frenzy! Anna Maria had been a Mille Miglia specialist since 1933, and had won her class in 1952 in the Eiffelrennen, but was disqualified for receiving outside help. This decision was highly criticized by the press, for, having had polio as a youngster, she could not push her vehicle by herself … An excellent Italian racing driver, Anna Maria drove everything, from the small Stanguellini 750 and the Maserati A6GS, to the big Ferrari 500TR.

1956 was to be Gilberte's best season, despite the tragedy, but also her last. Briefly, she won the first Tour de Corse with Nadège Ferrier in a small Dauphine Gordini (still with her beloved rear engine), ahead of a Porsche Carrera, Lageneste's Alfa Romeo, and Georges Houel's 300 SL. After one last race in the United States in 1957 (the Sebring 12-Hours in the same Dauphine Gordini), she hung up her helmet and married a wealthy Brussels industrialist. She was never to stray far from racing circles throughout the rest of her life, but never went back to racing, instead devoting herself to family life.

Gilberte Thirion, after a long and painful illness, was surrounded by her nearest and dearest until her final days. A beautiful old lady, whose life was filled with marvelous memories, her greatest regret was not having raced in the Le Mans 24-Hours in the Gordini T17S, in which she had qualified in trials. Under pressure from the ACO, and following the previous year's sporting tragedy, it was her father who had driven in the race. She died in May 2008.

1953 Tour Auto for Gilberte. Still fresh and smiling, at the end of a stage. (JFB Collection)

Gilberte and Lise Renaud in the seventh Tour de Belgique in 1955, with the official 4CV 1063. (Mertens Collection)

Gilberte Thirion at the Paris Mille Kilomètres on 10 June 1956, with Anna Peduzzi. They finished in 10th place. (Mertens Collection)

Annie Bousquet (1923-1956)

A pretty blonde, blue-eyed Austrian, Annie Scheffer had come into Pierre Bousquet's life while he was still a prisoner in Vienna. The only daughter of a well-off family, she had grown up enjoying tennis, music, horse-riding and skiing; Pierre brought her back to France and married her. He taught her to drive, but this still wasn't enough for this sporty young woman.

It was in 1952 in Sestrières, where Annie was recovering from a skiing accident, that she met Gigi Villoresi and Alberto Ascari in a hotel bar, and it was from this point that her destiny as a racing driver was decided. Fired with enthusiasm by the adventures of the two Italians, she decided, on the spot, to enter the first women's race, the Sestrière Rally, with Ascari, which is how the two champions became Annie's spiritual godfathers. Next came rallies in 4CVs, and a first Ladies' Cup in the Dauphine, after which she turned to a Porsche and undertook intensive training with Toto Veuillet, a Porsche importer, in order to understand its mechanics.

Annie was a girl with a bubbly personality and infectious enthusiasm, but also an overflowing schedule

(which was to prove fatal). In 1953, when driving a DB 500 racer in Agen, following a notorious racing driver in an effort to achieve a time, the cushion of her seat detached itself and she was thrown through the circuit fencing, resulting in a broken leg and hospitalisation. Hardly had she recovered from this than she was back with a vengeance. In 1955, she again broke a leg – at the wheel of a Porsche Spyder 550 – in the Agadir Grand Prix.

Annie often co-drove with her friend, Gilberte Thirion; they even bought a Gordini roadster, which they raced in the Mille Miglia, solo or together. However, the 1954 Tour de France automobile would be the end of their friendship. Rivals Gilberte and Ingeborg Polenski in a Porsche 356, and Annie with Marie Claire Beaulieu (daughter of Monsieur Cibié, the future Mrs Merenda) in a Spyder 550, were jostling for first place throughout the rally, combining a battle of nerves with propaganda via the intermediary of the press. Annie had chosen a roadster, as she preferred track racing, but driving in an open car was going to be tiring. She confided her impressions to *L'Équipe* magazine: "In this tour I had the devil against me. He chased us right from the

Annie Bousquet in a Porsche Spyder 550, before her record for the 1 hour at Montlhéry in August 1955, and just before her accident, due to tyre failure. (Bavouzet Collection)

Amédée Gordini, Gilberte, Max Thirion and Annie Bousquet in front of their Gordini roadster, which they had just bought together in 1954. They entered the Mille Miglia with this car. (Mertens Collection)

start," explained the blonde Annie, with a smile on her face. "On the road, we lost our helmets. In Rouen, a fan couldn't resist taking the toolbox. From Paris, the burst petrol tank flooded our knees and, in La Turbie, an oil pipe packed up, giving off so much smoke that we thought it would catch fire and almost jumped overboard!" Their misfortunes continued, and in Nice their door opened of its own accord at each bend ... She was also cursing, for the Gordinis of André Guelfi (alias 'Dédé the Sardine') and Jacky Pollet were locked in a fratricidal struggle and blocking their way. Pollet won the Tour. Annie and Marie Claire finished eighth overall and second of the ladies behind Gilberte, who was fifth! End of a friendship ...

Annie had big plans, and dreamed of doing the Pan-American in one of the green and white cars of a major French perfume producer. In 1955, she turned up at the start of the Monte Carlo with Lise Renaud and a Panhard Dyna. The cup was much contested that year, and Sheila Van Damm was desperately fighting for her second European championship title with her Sunbeam. With January 17 the start of the rally, everyone took advantage of the Christmas holiday to do some reconnaissance. Lise Renaud recalled: "It was Philippe Faure's car, prepared by the factory. The night of New Year's Eve, we took over four hours to get from Sisteron to Digne, which is an average of less than 38km/h (24mph).

Annie Bousquet at Spa on 23 May 1954. It often rains there ... (JFB Collection)

Entered once more in the 1956 Mille Miglia, but in a Triumph TR2, alone from beginning to end. (DR)

Annie Bousquet with her Gordini roadster, which she was to drive with Gilberte Thirion in the Mille Miglia. (Mertens Collection)

Annie Bousquet's last Porsche 550, damaged in the Rheims 12-Hours, in July 1956. (Mertens Collection)

It is true that it was past midnight and that the road was totally covered in black ice. I got out of the Panhard after it span around, and as soon as my feet touched the ground I was flat on my back! What an ice rink! All this effort was to be in vain. During the rally, the engine blew at Nogaro. We came back to Monaco by train."

Also in 1955, Annie made it onto the podium, finishing second in the Paris 24-Hours. She also launched into a record attempt on the Montlhéry circuit in a bid to beat that set by Gwenda Stewart-Hawkes and her Derby-Miller in 1934. She prepared her trusty little Spyder. Alas! On the 29th lap, just as all was running smoothly, she burst a rear tyre at 230km/h (143mph) and spun off the track. She mustered the strength to escape from the vehicle despite multiple fractures, and, on her hospital bed, declared that she would try again!

However, this was a bad year for motorsport. Levegh's accident at Le Mans cooled public enthusiasm, and the two seasons of 1955 and 1956 witnessed the loss of Alberto Ascari, Pierre Levegh, Donald Beauman, John Heath, Benoît Musy, and Louis Rosier. The sporting press was questioning the drivers' qualifications, with heavy insinuations about women racing drivers ...

The Suez crisis occurred in 1956, and this was a doubly tragic year for Annie, who lost her husband, Pierre Bousquet, in a road traffic accident near Saulieu. Fighting her grief, she took part in the Paris Mille Kilomètres in a Maserati 1500 with Alex de Tomaso, and alone in the Mille Miglia in a TR2. She bestowed all her love and attention on her young daughter, Heidi, who was only fourteen. One month later, disaster struck. Annie was trying to squeeze too much into a tight schedule. Perhaps also upset by the recent loss of her husband, she embarked on the Rheims 12-Hours with energy and excitement, sharing the wheel with Isabelle Haskell (who was to become Mrs de Tomaso). Annie took the first leg, but, in the fast bend before Muizon, she crossed the track. Her blue Porsche clipped the left edge, bounced across to the other side, and rolled over several times. Annie was found lifeless in the meadow alongside the circuit. Gilberte, driving in her Gordini, withdrew from the race immediately. Paul Frère, a great Porsche racer and stable companion, remembers with dismay the blow dealt that day: "Unfortunately, nobody apart from Annie was in any doubt that she would one day fall victim to her enthusiasm. Yet the last thing I expected was that those two hours spent with her the previous evening were to be the last, and that, for 12 whole hours these would be revived for me before my very eyes each time I passed her crippled car by the side of the road." Lise Renaud, the loyal rally team-mate of Gilberte and Annie, recalls that terrible time with feeling: "I'd just lent Annie my helmet when she was killed at Rheims."

Annie's fatal accident in the Rheims 12-Hours in July 1956 was a black day for the future of our female track racing drivers, and it was not until the arrival of Marie-Claude Beaumont and her Corvette in 1971 that another woman driver was seen at Le Mans.

Annie rests beside her husband in the little cemetery of Mames-la-Coquette. As the motto, inspired by d'Annunzio and painted on Tazio Nuvolari's racing Alfa Romeo, states: Dona e motori, gioi e dolori; Women and motors, joy and pain.

Denise McCluggage (1927-)

American Denise McCluggage was known for her love of Porsches – and her white helmet with red polka dots. Journalist, writer and racing driver, she accumulated trophies on three continents.

Born in Eldorado, she was a journalist at the age of twelve. After studying philosophy and political economics, and, being very sporty (she also loved skiing and parachuting), her job as a photo journalist led her to cover the trials of all the early post-war American races, which ran on roads or disused aerodromes: Watkins

Denise McCluggage, journalist and Porsche racer, in the United States. (Porsche Archives)

Claude Storez' Porsche, just before his accident. He put on tyres that were too big, which proved fatal. Like Annie Bousquet, he was killed on this same circuit during the Routes du Nord Rally in 1959. Annie Soisbault's back can be seen, in a jacket. (Soisbault Collection).

Three years on, in February 1959, on the same Rheims circuit, during the Routes du Nord Rally, Claude Storez was killed in an almost identical Speedster Zagato due to a bad choice of tyres. Annie Soisbault told us: "The evening before, in the fog, we helped Claude and Buchet out of a ditch. His front wing had got twisted and was rubbing the tyre. The next day, in a bid to leave us behind on the Rheims circuit, as he was in pole position, he had wanted to put on large-diameter tyres. The first time he braked, his wheel jammed in the wing, which was still twisted, and he rolled over into the ditch, colliding with a concrete post. A stupid accident! And yet we had told him about the tyres! Look, this is me in the photo on the right in a jacket. I've lost three friends because of badly adapted or worn-out tyres: the Marquis de Portago in the Mille Miglia, Henri Oreiller, who smashed his Ferrari GTO into the Dunlop cabin by the control tower at Montlhéry, and now him!"

Storez and his Porsche, starting in pole position. (JFB Collection)

A disastrous series for those Porsche Spyders, which were to kill many famous racing drivers (along with James Dean in his RSK, in 1955 on the road to Salinas … and Jean Behra at the Avus track in 1959). Fortunately, all went well for most of them. The English Jacqueline Evans, a naturalized Mexican, was to enjoy good luck in the five Pan-Americanas in her 356, and Denise McCluggage was to make her own contribution to the American victories of this same Porsche Spyder.

Right: The lethal signpost, which he hit in passing, before rolling into the ditch. (JFB Collection)

What remains of his poor Spyder 550. (JFB Collection)

Jacqueline Evans at the 1954 Carrera Panamericana, with a Porsche Carrera, of course. (Mertens Collection)

Glen, Beverly, Eagle Mountain, Elkhart Lake, Sebring and Nassau. Grand Prix had existed for a long time in Europe, but not yet in the United States. The end of the war had sent a good deal of sports-loving American soldiers home, often with a European sports car in their baggage, and this was all it took for the advent of those races that were to gain in importance over the 1950s and 1960s. Jaguar, MG, AC, Ferrari, Maserati, Gordini, and even the little Panhards which were renowned for their energy efficiency. All of those Americans from East and West Coasts would be united, during the dormant winter season of the European races, by the greatest champions such as Phil Hill, Stirling Moss, Olivier Gendebien, Fon de Portago, Peter Collins, Huschke von Hanstein, Musso, Bucci, Fangio, von Trips, and Bonnier, who were only too pleased to be able to continue training during the winter, and in idyllic surroundings.

Better structured, for a demanding public and media, the races were held in Nassau, Cuba, Caracas, and Puerto Rico. Denise McCluggage had the good fortune "to have been one of them." With her commentaries she covered the whole of this golden age where the greatest racing drivers were all accessible, sitting on a stack of tyres or on a low wall before the race (read her excellent book *American Racing*, with its extraordinary photos). Better still, she shared the wheel of those drivers who became her friends. As she had a knack with the steering wheel, she naturally won many Ladies' Cups. Her best memories are of Sebring in 1961, in a Ferrari 250 GT, and the Monte Carlo in a massive Ford Falcon.

Also a well-known journalist in Europe, she raced and tested all sorts of sports cars such as Lotus, Osca, Maserati, Jaguar, and Mini Cooper, and her name is now inscribed in the *Automotive Hall of Fame*. She is enjoying a none-too-quiet retirement, for she continues to write for numerous magazines and internet pages, in and around Santa Fe.

Denise McCluggage's Porsche 550 in Caracas, in the 1957 Venezuela Grand Prix. (Porsche Archives)

Denise's Spyder 550 in action at the 1957 Caracas Grand Prix. (Porsche Archives)

Betty Skelton (1926-)

Betty was a daredevil who flew a plane solo at the age of 12 and passed her pilot's licence at sixteen. On the track, she was the first woman to have driven in a race at Indianapolis. Yet, in true Anglo-Saxon style, the Americans were as prone to prevarication as the British when it came to women racing drivers; as they used to say, women were not 'encouraged' to race.

In 1964, Betty Skelton – a young, single brunette – was a brilliant publicity manager at Campbell Ewell Company, and looked after the Chevrolet marque's advertising. To promote the brand, she organized rallies in which the goal was to get from the East to the West Coast – she made it in 56 hours, 58 minutes, and crossings by car of the Andes Cordillera. She set a record in a Corvette at Daytona Beach in 1956, at over 145mph (233km/h), also passed all the tests for being an astronaut, and went on to fly helicopters and jets. This led her, in 1965, to a record attempt on the salt lake of Bonneville in a Green Monster Cyclops (a record-breaking vehicle propelled by an F86-Sabre jet), where she broke the 277.62mph (446.79km/h) record! She also had a career as an aerobatic pilot! Her name is now inscribed in the Chevrolet Corvette Pilot Hall of Fame.

Betty Skelton, advertising executive, pilot, and speed record holder on the track. She also entered numerous races at Daytona Beach in a Corvette. (DR)

Betty Skelton breaking the 277mph (445.8km/h) record in her Cyclops, on 27 September 1965. (Blanchet Collection)

Betty Skelton at the wheel of the green monster Cyclops for the 277mph (445.8km/h) record in 1965. (Blanchet Collection)

5

St Tropez, mini skirts and Mini Cooper

Over 15 years had elapsed since the war. The motoring industry had metamorphosed, as had its associated sport. Fangio had retired after 80 victories. Bardot had become engaged to Sacha Distel, then married Jacques Charrier. Anita Eckberg dived into the Trevi Fountain and the Berlin Wall was erected. Then there was the Cold War in the east, assassination of Kennedy in the west, and everything else that was going on in-between with the Algerian war, Vietnam, de Gaulle and the Beatles. For two French authors, the decade accelerated in a Facel-Vega on the N5 road (Marcel Camus), and exploded in an E-Type Jaguar on the Normandy autoroute (Jean Bruce). Perspectives were shattered. The new wave had arrived and, with it, a new wave of racing drivers, too.

The

1960s

The 1960s. Sunbeam Alpine at Earl's Court in 1961. (JFB Collection)

Françoise Sagan (1935-2004)

Just joking, of course! Françoise was never a racing driver, even though she did pose proudly, sitting on her Gordini roadster, which was, in fact, only hers for 10 days, as it was just a huge publicity stunt by Amédée Gordini senior and 'Dédé the Sardine' (alias André Guelfi), who was to compete with it in the Paris Mille Kilomètres.

Françoise was not to receive the car until after the race, although she could have been a racing driver and raced the Paris-Saint-Raphaël Rally like all those before her. After all, she already drove barefoot and at top speed down to the Côte d'Azur in one night to have her breakfast at the Café Sénéquier, and smashed up a few Jaguars and Astons. "I prefer to cry in my Jaguar rather than in a bus," she explained.

The epicentre of the new wave was between the Café de Flore in the Rue Saint-Benoit and the Deux Magots at the Saint-Germain crossroad, from where the Paris-St Tropez rally started: watch out for the gendarmes!

During this period, the French automobile industry overtook the millionth car mark, and was advised to "put a tiger in your tank."

October 1957. Françoise Sagan has had an accident in an Aston Martin, and was to have several more ... Bonjour Tristesse! Its beautiful aluminium coachwork ... (JFB Collection)

The Gordini belonging to Françoise Sagan and 'Dédé the Sardine,' alias André Guelfi. Françoise drove it in the Paris Mille Kilomètres. (JFB Collection)

Louisette Texier (1925-)

This dynamic slip of a girl and shrewd businesswoman (she owned ready-to-wear boutiques in Neuilly) never took a holiday except to enter rallies! Extremely fit, at Shell she was called 'the Bulldozer' or even 'Le Louisette,' referring to an early nickname for the guillotine. Nothing could stop her. At the Charbonnières, she did 800 kilometres (497 miles) in rain with a smashed windscreen, finishing third overall. Once, everything did stop: "In 1961 I did a Tour de France with a novice, Mrs Mermod, and I didn't want to hand over the wheel to her. I had driven 7000 kilometres (4350 miles) on the trot, and was winning my class. The finish was at Ajaccio, then in Nice. I let her take the wheel to take the car to the boat. A flock of sheep suddenly appeared at a bend; she panicked and rolled our poor Alfa Giulietta TI into the ditch." A compound fracture of the arm for Louisette and the end of the road for the Alfa. It was Claudine Vanson (the future Mrs Trautmann) who was to win with her ID 19.

Her racing career started at Montlhéry. Louisette, being the typical Armenian that she was, had succeeded in business, and was, therefore, one of those rare women to own a car. Ever somewhat impecunious, her friend, Georges Houel, asked her to take him one Sunday to Montlhéry to watch his friend, Georges Monnaret, driving. There, they came across Jean Behra, who expounded to Louisette the joys of rallying. A few months later, in 1956, she set off for the 16th Monte Carlo with a veteran: Germaine Rouault.

On meeting her a few days earlier, at the Action Automobile bar in the Avenue d'Lena, Jojo Houel thrust a young girl towards her as a team-mate for the Ladies' Cup – a team of three earns more points! This was a certain Annie Soisbault ... Pat Moss, another promising youngster, accompanied Mrs Jones in an Austin A90 on

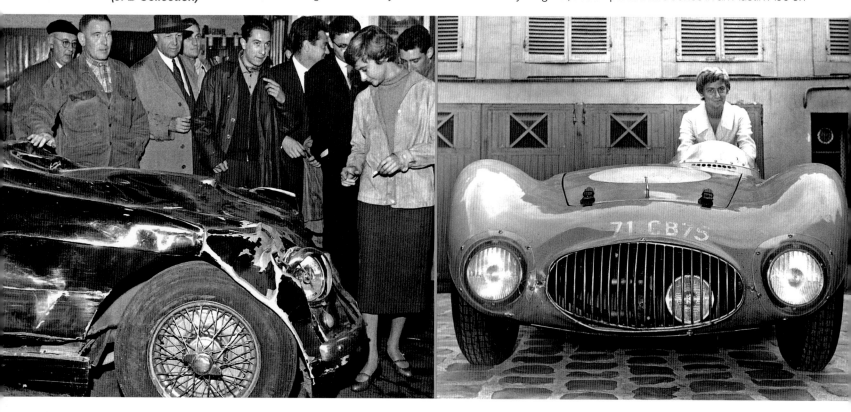

Far left: The 'new wave'
having a laugh between
Paris and St Tropez.
(JFB Collection)

'Put a tiger in your tank,'
screams the advert!
(JFB Collection)

The first Monte Carlo Rally
for Louisette Texier and
Annie Soisbault, in 1956.
They were accompanied
by veteran Germaine
Rouault. There were
three of them in the
Simca Aronde. It was
a modest result – 119th
out of 233 ranked – but
they made it to the end.
(Texier Collection)

Right: Louisette Texier in 1956; photo by Studio Harcourt. (Texier Collection)

Georges Houel. The man who 'made it all happen' for Louisette Texier, Annie Soisbault and Corinne Koppenhague. The type of guy you bump into in the Bar de L'Action in the Avenue d'Iéna and gives you the racing bug. (JFB Collection)

The Alfa ended up damaged in the 1961 Tour Auto, with Marie Louise 'Poupette' Mermod at the wheel, avoiding a flock of sheep. (Louche Collection)

this 1956 Monte Carlo. Louisette Texier was not going to cause an upset on the scoreboard, with their gallant Simca Aronde achieving a sedate 119th place (out of 233 finishers), but they made it to the end and she was delighted with that. She would try again. Gilberte Thirion was to be placed 40th, and second of the ladies' in her small 4CV.

Louisette learnt quickly and took part in numerous rallies. She raced an Alfa TI and won the 1960 Lyons-Charbonnières rally with Annie Soisbault, sharing with her the Louis d'ors (French coins) that came with the cup. She won the 1964 Tourisme du Tour Auto Ladies' Cup with her Jaguar Mk2, still with Mrs Mermod. Louisette was as good at navigating as she was at driving, and enjoyed a fine career with Annie Soisbault, whom she chaperoned like a mother. Moreover, in that same year of 1964, when Annie was not with Louisette, she also won the Ladies' Cup in GT racing with her Ferrari GTO.

Returning to the Tour Auto, Louisette – who is by nature generous and honest – was leading her class with her Jaguar. She reached the checkpoint somewhere in the Alpes-de-Haute Provence, which was miles from anywhere, checked in and picked up two logbooks instead of one; the other belonged to Vic Elford, whose team-mate had simply forgotten to pick it up. Their Cortina Lotus was no longer anywhere to be seen. At the next checkpoint, Louisette found the co-driver, looking drawn – as far as he was concerned, the rally was over. She handed him the logbook, to the disgust of Masoero who was a few seconds behind Elford! Final scratch positions: 3rd Consten, 4th Elford, 5th Masoero, 6th Texier!

In fact, Bernard Consten was a friend of Louisette and they both drove Jaguar Mk2s. He was also a practical joker: in every hillclimb heat of this rally, unbeknown to Louisette, he filled her boot with baggage in a bid to gain seconds!

Louisette raced the Tour d'Europe once more with Lise Renaud. "This wasn't a rally for weaklings! We withstood fatigue better than the men and our vanity was perhaps the best of weapons, for we did all we could to get ahead of schedule in order to stop, freshen up, re-do our make-up and hair, and clock in at the checkpoints as fresh as daisies!"

Louisette Texier, Lise Renaud, Régine Gordine and Gilberte Thirion all raced or navigated together, and were great friends off the track. Lise was godmother to Sacha, the son of Régine Gordine, and to Gilberte Thirion's daughter. Annie Soisbault was the baby of the gang.

Louisette and Monique Bouvier in the Mobil Economy Run. In August 1956 they arrived safely at Hyères in their Versailles, sporting Hermes scarves. (JFB Collection)

Annie Soisbault, Marquise de Montaigu (1934-)

Her motto was 'au danger, mon plaisir,' which means 'oh to live dangerously!'

Annie Blanche Marie was born in the Rue Cimarosa, to a lawyer father and a mother who was a doctor. Ultra-sportiing, she was the seven-times junior and intermediate tennis champion of France, and even reached a Wimbledon final in 1953. At 14 she could drive her mother's electric car, and at 16 had a scooter, which she modified to make it go faster. During her English degree course, she did casual work (selling fridges) to earn the cash to buy herself a powerful car, for Annie was already mad about speed. This was a Delahaye Grand Sport cabriolet, which was beautiful, but guzzled the petrol and frequently broke down. All her tennis prize money was spent on it, but her holidays on the coast were going to be fabulous!

When she came of age, her godmother gave her a beautiful red TR3, and it was at the wheel of this that she met Georges Houel one evening on the Champs Élysées. "We went out for dinner with his friends: Harry Schell (the son of Lucy and Laurie), José Behra (Jean's brother), Germaine Rouault and Louisette Texier." She was about to find herself embarking on her first Monte Carlo Rally with these last two, as a passenger on the back seat. "I was in a tracksuit and trainers, with all 5ft 9in of me stretched out in the back and banned from touching the steering wheel. I was only allowed to 'belt up.' When we got to Ardèche, there was a snowstorm. Seeing that we were getting further and further behind schedule, I asked to drive. They didn't want to know. At Vienne, I told them I would get out if they didn't let me drive. 'Well my dear, if you think you're such an expert, we'll hand you the joystick!' [Germaine Rouault's banter]. I caught up with nearly all the competitors. When we

Annie Soisbault, navigated by Louisette, won the 1963 Tour Auto Ladies' Cup. Better still, they came second in the scratch race, just behind Bernard Consten. (Soisbault Collection).

A happy Annie Soisbault, at the wheel of her new TR3 in 1959. (Soisbault Collection).

reached the next stop, the Shell racing director, Guy de Beaumont, came to congratulate them. Silence ... then: 'It was the kid who was driving ...' replied Germaine" and that was how Annie became known.

She was also to accompany Monique Bouvier in her Panhard to the 1957 Mille Miglia 'just to watch.' Their number was just after that of Paul Frère's Dauphine. Unfortunately, they were to run a big end.

But 1957 also saw her first real rally with her TR3, at the Tour de Corse. With Germaine Rouault as co-driver, she finished fourth overall, behind Lageneste's Alfa and two Porsches, and won the Ladies' Cup – her first cup!

In June 1957, Annie took part in a Dauphine Renault ladies' race at Montlhéry, where she won again, ahead of all her colleagues. Then came the Tour Auto in a TR3 with Michèle Cancre, and another Ladies' Cup.

Annie Soisbault was now feared and respected by her peers. Ken Richardson, head of the Triumph competition department, noticed her and offered her a place as a works driver. For her first Tulip Rally in 1958, she was lumbered with an English chaperone, Pat Ozane, who made a mistake in her notes. Annie removed her from the Triumph by the collar ... and left her at the roadside!

In 1959, she set her sights on the title of European female rally champion, which she won equally with Ewy Rosqvist, the Swedish Volvo queen. In 1960 she started the Monte Carlo Rally with the brand new Triumph Herald, Anne Spears and Cheeta – her cheetah – on the back seat. This was a huge publicity stunt and after the start Annie gave it to her mother, who had to return it to her at the finish. Throughout the rally, the press thought that the cheetah was sleeping under the blanket and guarding the car. In fact, it was Annie who slept in the paddock, and complained vehemently when disturbed ... Pat Moss and Anne Wisdom were to win the Ladies' Cup that year in their Austin A40.

Annie was the darling of the jet set, spending winter in Megève and summer in St Tropez with friends such as Bob Westhoff (who had married Françoise Sagan), Karajan, Chazot, Régine, Debarge, and Bardot. She raced her Jaguar Mk2 and competed against the greatest, often teamed with Bernard Consten. She won the La Baule Rally, which was where, at a checkpoint at 6 o'clock in the morning, she met another competitor, the Marquis de Montaigu, who was immediately attracted to "a girl who ran on white wine and bacon omelette when everyone else was taking coffee." This was the beginning of an unshakable collaboration. The divine marquis was a fervent admirer of her driving and her laidback manner, and courted her relentlessly, smothering her with gifts. They married in the town hall of the 16th arrondissement in Paris (five minutes after the marriage of a tall pale boy with protruding ears: a certain Serge Gainsbourg!).

The marquis gave Annie ever more extraordinary cars in which she continued to sweep the board at rallies. She wasn't interested in the Ladies' Cups; an outright win was what she was after, and she got it. She even won at Monza in 1964 ahead of Enzo Ferrari, who grabbed hold of her at the finish and kissed her! Annie used to beat the male racing drivers and threaten their male ego. Moreover, she was the target of sabotage attempts: sugar in the petrol, an unbolted wheel, oil removed from the axle ... but her fiery temperament spurred her on even more to encounter glory at the greatest time in the history of car rallies.

If she skidded in a pool of oil on Mont Ventoux in 1960 with her GTO, she took her revenge in 1966 with a Porsche 906, and was the first woman to exceed an average speed of 100km/h (62mph).

Start of the 1956 Monte Carlo Rally, Annie's first rally. From right to left: Germaine Rouault, Simone Soisbault, Annette Englebert, Annie Soisbault and Louisette Texier. (Soisbault Collection)

Annie in the 1957 Mille Miglia with Monique de Bouvier's Panhard. They were to run a big end. (Soisbault Collection)

Renault promotional races at Montlhéry. The draw for the cars on 16 June 1957. Annie started with No 139 and won the race ahead of Monique Bouvier, although they had planned to cross the line together. (JFB Collection)

Start of the race at Montlhéry. (Patrimoine Renault Archives)

Annie first and Monique Bouvier second. (Patrimoine Renault Archives)

Left: In 1958, Annie became the works driver with Triumph and signed a contract with Ken Richardson. VHP 529, Ken's service TR3, is parked in front of the Bar de l'Action, where it all happened in motor racing in the 1960s. Annie was pleased and her season was a success. (Soisbault Collection)

Previous page, top to bottom and left to right:

After the 1957 Tour de Corse, where she came fourth in the scratch race, Annie entered the Tour Auto with her TR3. She won the Ladies' Cup with Michèle Cancre. Well done, girls! (Soisbault Collection)

1958 Monte Carlo with Pat Ozane. Sent off-course in a blizzard, she fared much better later on. (Soisbault Collection)

1959 Tour Auto. With Michèle Cancre, Ladies' Cup in the bag. (Soisbault Collection)

1959 Portugal Rally with Renée Wagner. The TR3 is the 1959 Monte Carlo ex-Gatsonides. (Soisbault Collection)

Cheeta the cheetah at Annie's home in the Rue Cimarosa, Paris. (JFB Collection)

1960 Monte Carlo with Anne Spiers. The year of the cheetah and the Triumph Herald. 125th overall, but a huge media coup for the cheetah. (JFB Collection)

1960 Tour de France auto with a Porsche S90. Briefing at Montlhéry with Jo Schlesser in a Ferrari, Bartholoni in a DB, Willy Mairesse in a 250 GT, Annie Soisbault in a Porsche, La Geneste in a 250 GT, and Berney in a 250 GT. (JFB Collection)

The 1960 Mont Ventoux hillclimb race in a Ferrari GTO. An unmarked pool of oil ruins her efforts. She was to get her revenge six years later with a Porsche 906, when she exceeded the 100km/h (62mph) average barrier. (Soisbault Collection)

1960 Tour Auto. Annie, Michèle Cancre and Virgil Conrero, the Alfa Romeo wizard. (Soisbault Collection)

1962 Paris-Saint-Raphaël. Annie, her Jaguar Mk2 TDF, Nicole Roure and Louisette Texier. (Soisbault Collection)

The Salon de Paris. The Garage Mirabeau Aston Martin stand where Annie is deep in conversation with Richard Anthony and his wife, in 1965. Will they be leaving in an Aston? (Soisbault Collection)

She partnered exceptional women, such as showjumping champion Michèle Cancre (wife of the Chevalier d'Orgeix); stopwatch queens Renée Wagner and Michèle Dubosc; Lise Renaud, always ahead of the field with her make-up; Nicole Roure, Régine Gordine, Louisette Texier (the Bulldozer), and Monte Carlo veteran Germaine Rouault. At the beginning of 1969, with an impressive string of achievements under her belt, Annie hung up her gloves and helmet to become the high-powered managing director of the Garage Mirabeau, devoting herself to importing Aston Martins, Jaguars and Triumphs. "After ten years of racing and winning, I felt like doing something else. I launched the fashion for London taxis outside the Castel et Régine nightspot. I sold dozens of Mini Coopers to the whole of the jet set and to my friend's mistresses. They were, in fact, rented and, when they split up, I used to send a chauffeur to pick up the keys! Oh, the tears!"

From time to time, and to escape from the office, she dabbled in small races and would be seen at Mont Ventoux, Dakar, or even the Angola Grand Prix, just for fun.

"It was I who inspired David Brown with the new Aston abbreviation of that time. He had come to renegotiate my importation contract and we were celebrating at Maxim's. He was looking for a name for his new model. His wife's name was Suzann, which made her initials SDB. I turned it into DBS and that idea stuck! I used to do a lot of hunting at that time and had

Annie in St Tropez with her husband, the Marquis de Montaigu, and Annabelle Buffet. (Soisbault Collection)

the idea of asking him to make an Aston Break to be able to put my guns in. A week later, I had an Italian designer in my garage, and David Brown produced a few Aston Breaks! In a word, we had a lot of fun at that time. My husband, the Marquis, held heaps of parties and our lives were surrounded by writers, artists and political personalities. During the summer, at the Place des Lices in St Tropez, we used to play boules with Richard Anthony, Juliette Gréco, Eddy Barclay, Johnny Hallyday, Antoine, Collaro, Carlos, Just Jaeckin and Brigitte Bardot. What a life!"

One could carry on listening for hours to these anecdotes of such a full life. Nowadays, Annie lives quietly in her Neuilly apartment, very much surrounded by her friends, who come regularly to taste her home-made foie gras, as she is just as handy with a saucepan as she is at the wheel!

Ewy Rosqvist, Baroness von Korf

In 1959, Ewy was the woman Annie Soisbault had to beat. Both excellent, they finished up equal. Ewy was born on a farm in Ystad in Sweden, and studied to be a vet. Like Annie, she was a very good tennis player. A racing fanatic, spotted by Volvo, she was very soon taken on to race, which she did for three years, winning the first European championship, along with those in 1960 and 1961 for Mercedes. She also went on to win the Argentina road race Grand Prix, 5500 kilometres (3417.5 miles) across the Pampas with a Mercedes in 1962. She is the only woman to have been an official racing driver for Mercedes. Ewy lives in Stockholm, and is now Baroness von Korf.

Pat Moss (1934-2008)

The best known English woman driver of her kind was Pat Moss, with a brother who was already famous, and a husband, Erik Carlsson, who was as well known as she. Sister to Stirling, Pat already had a recognisable surname, but was to later earn herself a nickname. Her father, Alf Moss, raced on circuits (Indianapolis, 1924) and her mother raced in trials and rallies. An inveterate sportswoman, along with her friend, Anne Wisdom (the daughter of Elsie and Tom Wisdom), she was a successful horsewoman. She passed her driving test at seventeen, and in 1953 made up the rally team with Ken Gregory, Stirling's manager.

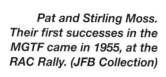

Then she had a go with a Morris Minor she had just bought. This was a revelation. Marcus Chambers, BMC's brand new racing manager, spotted her and offered her an MG for the RAC Rally in 1955. The first performance was hardly convincing, and then she overturned an Austin Westminster in the 1956 Monte Carlo. Matters soon improved and a partnership with Anne Wisdom began: for seven years they swept the board (Anne went on to marry and give up racing, and Pat also got married, but to a racing driver, and continued with a vengeance).

Meanwhile, 'Mossie and Wizz' – as they were dubbed – made their debuts at the Liège-Rome-Liège in 1957 in a Morris 1000, then in an Austin A40 at the

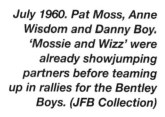

1959 and 1960 Monte Carlo rallies. Their Austin was called 'Zoe' because its registration number was 'XOE 778,' then 'Zokky' for 'XOK 195,' they always gave their cars names. There was also 'URX,' the red Big Healey of the Alpine Cup.

The 1958 season got under way in an MGA, then with the new Big Healeys, which became her brand image. From 1958 to 1962, they took part in twenty rallies in a row, achieving eleven victories. They were to win the scratch race in the 1960 Liège-Rome-Liège and the Tulip Rally in 1962. Pat was a terrific smoker, and she chain-smoked as much as Annie Soisbault in rallies, which is why she always travelled with her legendary enormous handbag!

Anne went on to marry Peter Riley and fell pregnant in 1962, announcing that she was going to give up racing. This was a disappointment for Pat, who had to find another team-mate – Pauline Mayman. This partnership worked well, but it was not the same, although she nevertheless secured a third victory in the 1962 European championship. In 1963, Pat married the champion Erik Carlsson, whose Swedish nickname was 'På taket' (on the roof ...). She then went on to race for Saab, securing a fifth place in the Monte Carlo.

Pat took part in rallies until 1975 when – a little-known fact – she carried off several cups for the Alpine marque. She won a fine Ladies' Cup in a Berlinette 1600 S at the 1972 Monte Carlo. For a long time Pat helped her daughter, Suzie, with her showjumping, and took great delight in driving her enormous Scania van. Active right until the end, she died after a long illness at the age of 73.

As time went by, the more the competition for the Ladies' Cup intensified in the rallies of the 1960s. At least 10 female teams would appear at the start of each Monte Carlo rally, Tour de France auto, or Tour de Corse, and a wave of Englishwomen monopolized the Ladies' Cups. Amongst the most famous was Annie Hall, who drove her own Jaguar XK 120 to the RAC, winning the Ladies' Cup, going on to drive for Sunbeam with Sheila Van Damm, then in an Anglia for Ford, in a Zephyr in the East African Safari, followed by Mercedes and Rovers. Rosemary Smith had no inclination whatsoever to enter rallies. She was a dress designer in her own business. It was Liz Bigger, wife of Jaguar racing driver, Frank Bigger, who recruited her to navigate in a rally. As Rosemary was not very good with maps, Liz handed over the wheel, with rather good results. She tried again. Spotted by the boss of Rootes, she joined the team and became famous through her Hillman Imp in the 1965 Alpine Cup, in which she won the ladies' award. She also won the scratch in the 1965 Tulip Rally, ahead of 165 competitors. She raced for Porsche and did a London-Sydney with Lucette Pointet in a Ford Cortina. During the '70s she drove pretty much everything, including BMWs, Minis, and Datsuns. She now lives in Dublin and still races in historic car rallies.

Annie Hall and Mrs Domleo in the 1960 Monte Carlo, in a Ford Anglia. They were to finish 36th overall. (JFB Collection)

Below, left: Rosemary Smith. (JFB Collection)

Rosemary Smith in the 1965 Tulip Rally in a Hillman Imp. (JFB Collection)

Initiation to rallying with the famous little Austin A40 named Zoe (XOE 778), preparing for the 1959 Monte Carlo Rally. (JFB Collection)

The 1962 season in a Big Healey. 26 May 1962, the Acropolis Rally. (JFB Collection)

1960 Alpine Cup. Victory for Anne Wisdom and URX 727. (Chevalier Collection)

A less well-documented time for Pat Moss was when she was driving Team Aseptogyl Alpines in 1972, and won the Monte Carlo Ladies' Cup with new team-mate Liz Crellin. Anne Wisdom had become Mrs Peter Riley. (JFB Collection)

Claudine Bouchet, Vanson, Trautmann (1931-)

To compete with this wave of British Racing Green in the 1960s, few Frenchwomen remained at the top of the ladder after Annie Soisbault left in 1965, although Claudine Trautmann was there with Lucette Pointet and their famous Citroën DSs, along with Marie-Claude Beaumont in an Opel GT and Chevrolet Camaro.

Claudine Bouchet worked in her father's clock-making business in the Grenoble area and, until the age of 24, had had no contact with the world of rallying.

A friend who was a Simca dealer persuaded her to enter the Mont Blanc Rally. She won the Ladies' Cup and came fourth in the scratch race, ahead of the Porsches and Alfas … She was also at the 1959 and 1960 Monte Carlo rallies. She married a journalist and became Mrs Vanson. Then René Cotton, from Citroën, spotted her and took her on in an ID19. Claudine was four times champion of France, and won the Ladies' Cup in Corsica three times.

Claudine met René Trautmann at Citroën, its star racing driver, and he became her second husband. They often raced together and she followed him to Lancia in 1964, where she experienced the finest part of her racing career. In 1970, she took part in the London-Mexico in a DS 21, and was recruited by Bob Neyret to drive an Alpine for the female Aseptogyl team. She eventually became team manager for the entire stable. She was nine times French rally champion, raced from 1971 to 1973, and took part in the Bandama, the Ivory Coast and Moroccan rallies. These days Claudine lives in the Périgord, where she cooks and paints.

Colette Bouchet's debut at the 1960 Monte Carlo in her Simca P60, with Ginette Derolland. They achieved a modest 38th place. (JFB Collection)

Colette Trautmann followed René, her husband, to Lancia, where she had a fine career as a racing driver. Here she is with Catherine Piot in the 1968 Paris-Saint-Raphaël in a Lancia HF. (JFB Collection)

London-Mexico in a DS 21, with Colette Perrier, on 19 April 1970. (JFB Collection)

Colette Trautmann, team manager of the 1971 Team Asptogyl, for Bob Neyret. After also racing Alpines, she went on to manage them. (JFB Collection)

Lucette Pointet and Simone Petit

Lucette Pointet, known above all for her successes with Citroën, had started off with Simone Petit in a Dauphin 1093. Equally good at driving and navigating, she began at Citroën by helping Claude Ogier, and driving in a DS 19 and 21. She won the Ladies' Cup at the East African Safari in 1965, took part in the London-Sydney with Rose Mary Smith in a Cortina, and won the Ladies' Cup at the 1966 Monte Carlo in a DS 21. She had a successful career with Citroën and married Claude Ogier. She stopped racing during the 1970s. Lucette and Claude still live in the Grenoble area.

Simone Petit had a racing driver husband (Paul) who was very involved in the Association Sportive Automobile in his area (Grémieu, in the Isère). Nothing happens by chance in motorsport, and there is often a link between people, events and cars, so it was logical that Simone Petit should also race, and this she did in Renaults, Alfa Romeos and Gordinis. Incidentally, a great many female drivers raced the famous R8 'Gord'; Sylvia Osterberg won with the ladies at the 1967 Monte Carlo, and Lise Renaud, a 4CV veteran, also went back to the R8.

Lucette Pointet, an excellent Citroën racing driver. She won the 1966 Monte Carlo Ladies' Cup in a DS 21. (Louche Collection)

Simone Petit, a rally driver from Lyons, with her R8 Gordini. She won the Ladies' Cup at the 1967 Charbonnières. (JFB Collection)

Amazon Rally in Greece. Fifty fashion models posed along the route. The winners were Mrs Griva and Mrs Caffiri in a DS 19, in October 1966. (JFB Collection)

Far left: Sylvia Osterberg in an R8 Gordini at the 1967 Monte Carlo. (JFB Collection)

Lise Renaud in an R8 G. 1966 Fiori Rally. (JFB Collection)

Women racing drivers didn't only race in rallies, they also made a name for themselves on the track, even if the competition was tougher, with short sharp bursts of physical effort the order of the day. Olga Kevelos drove the Racer 500 against Stirling Moss; Ann Helm drove buses during the week, but appeared in Formula Ford racing at weekends. Several other young Englishwomen fought it out for the podiums. Anita Taylor specialized in the Ford Anglia, along with Gill Fortescue Thomas. Jill Robinson and Liz Jones were in Minis. The fastest and also the most modest of them was, undisputably, Christabel Carlisle: never was a girl so speedy in a Mini!

Pit-board signalling – with a flourish. (Male or female?) (JFB Collection)

Top: Ann Helms in Formula Ford, 1971. (JFB Collection)

Middle: Olga Kevelos in a Kieft Racer 500 at Brands Hatch. (JFB Collection)

Bottom: Anita Taylor and her Anglia at Brands Hatch in 1963. (DR)

Top left: Anita Taylor, aged 23, Ford Anglia driver and sister of F1 Lotus racing driver, Trevor Taylor. (JFB Collection)

Gill Fortescue Thomas drove both Minis and Ford Escorts. (DR)

Top: Jill Robinson in a Mini. (JFB Collection)

Liz Jones in a Mini Cooper. (JFB Collection)

Christabel Carlisle (1939-)

Christabel Carlisle behind the wheel, and Baroness Lady Watson in town! In 1960, Christabel Carlisle was a piano teacher, and her parents gave her an Austin Mini 850. By chance, some friends dragged her one Sunday to the Brands Hatch circuit. There, she was so bored she swore that, if she ever went back there, it would be on the track, behind the wheel. She was 21 and as good as her word, secretly entering a race with her little standard Mini. At the first turn, she ended up in a bale of hay. End of race ...

Christabel invested in lessons and listened to advice, and was very soon noticed by Marcus Chambers from BMC (as was Annie Soisbault). Supported by the racing department, she took part in her first real national race at Silverstone in 1961, but rolled over in practice. Her car was rebuilt overnight and she finished fifth in her class and twelfth overall. Not bad, but not good enough.

At Aintree in October she was second in her class, just behind Vic Elford. Bingo! She signed a contract with Castrol and BMC.

"I thought I was allowed to win, ahead of the cars in the John Cooper stable. In April, at Aintree, I dodged in and out between John Whitmore and Tony Maggs to finish in third place, thus preventing an all-Cooper podium. They have made me pay for it in every race since. No question of gentlemen drivers on the track. I was shoved and obstructed at the bends. It was awful!"

Christabel became the fastest girl in a Mini, coming second again at Brands Hatch behind Steve McQueen! She covered all the race tracks in Europe, still in her famous Mini with its personalized number plate 'CMC 77.' She took part in the 1963 Monte Carlo in an Austin-Healey with Makinen, coming 13th overall – despite the additional problem of a language barrier (Makinen neither spoke nor understood English). But Christabel, who had reached the peak of her racing, was to exit the track violently at Silverstone, putting a sudden end to her career.

The atmosphere in racing was changing and, with the arrival of sponsors, the money became more important than the sport. Christabel, who had become Lady Watson, hung up her helmet; with her, the history of amateur racing drivers turned a new page.

However, for a dynamic woman like her, life didn't stop there. At 50, she set off to trek all over the world, and climbed the Himalayas and Mount Ararat. She has walked to Santiago de Compostella, and from Land's End to John O'Groats.

A life member of the famous Cod Fillet stable, Christabel lives quietly in her manor in the south of England, tending her garden.

Right: Christabel Carlisle at the 1963 Monte Carlo with Makinen in a Healey 3000. (Chevalier Collection)

Bottom right: Christabel Carlisle, aged 22, at Brands Hatch in 1961 with a Mini Cooper. (JFB Collection)

Christabel Carlisle and her favourite Mini, CMC 77. (JFB Collection)

In Italy, the girls found it harder to make an impression: rare were those who had access to big red cars, and not just to the door of the kitchen. Rosadele Facetti was the daughter of one of Fangio's racing car mechanics. She also had a brother, and they both took part in the same disciplines, with the best man winning. This arrangement ended badly during a Temporada Argentina race at Mar del Plata when Rosa missed a bend and smashed into the crowd in her Tecno F3.

Rosadele Facetti after an accident at the Temporada Argentina in F3 at Mar del Plata, in February 1967. (JFB Collection)

Italian racing driver, Rosadele Facetti, in a Corvette in 1967. (JFB Collection)

6

The
1970s

The 1970s was the decade of the consumer society, where publicity ruled and circumstances were to completely change the atmosphere and practice of motor racing. Without a sponsor, you simply didn't stand a chance. At the same time, women's lib (and the arrival of tights …) created new opportunities for our tarmac heroines, who, once again, had an image to sell, and were at last accepted at Le Mans after a twenty-year absence. The main mechanical issues of those years were the battle between Ferrari, Ford, Porsche and Matra at Le Mans; the dominance in rallies of the small Alpine saloons, and the emergence of a new type of cross-country race: the Paris-Dakar. The years of female motorsport participation were marked by three significant events: involvement of a pretty blonde with a massive macho car in the Le Mans 24-Hours, that of a determined and attractive brunette in the French rally championship, and, finally, creation of the Team Aseptogyl, comprising a band of young girls in strawberry pink racing cars; in other words: Marie-Claude Beaumont and her Chevrolet Corvette, Michèle Mouton in an Alpine Renault and, finally, the team of dentist racing driver Bob Neyret, with all that was most glamorous and most efficient on wheels.

March 1970. The new liberated woman and the new Citroën SM. (JFB Collection)

Marie-Claude Beaumont (1941-)

In keeping with the image of a liberated woman of her era, Marie-Claude Beaumont was able to try out all the motorsport disciplines on offer at the time: rallies, track championships, Le Mans, and the rally raids in Africa. This pretty, resolute young woman was set to become an icon and a role model for women of the seventies.

Marie-Claude Charmasson was born in Grenoble, a town surrounded by mountains, where rallying means something to every lover of motorsport. Her father, Mr Charmasson, had a Citroën garage in nearby Gap, and did rallies in tuned Tractions. He took part in the Monte Carlo with his '15' and finished in third place.

The whole family would attend, of course, so Marie-Claude was immersed from an early age in the Citroën rallying ambience, whose works team used their garage as a support base. She even bumped into Paddy Hopkirk there, whose Mini Cooper had broken down during his Monte Carlo reconnaissance. On being sent to England to learn English, she saw Pat Moss racing at Silverstone one day; a real eye-opener.

In 1964, Claudine Trautmann gave Marie-Claude the chance to accompany her in a Routes du Nord rally. She won the Ladies' Cup. Two months later, in a Lancia, they covered the 5000 kilometres (3107 miles) in four days of dust in the Liège-Sofia-Liège. Then, in order not to embarrass her Citroën agent of a father, she adopted a pseudonym and henceforth called herself 'Beaumont.' In 1965, she won the La Baule with Henri Greder in a Mustang.

Her future lay with the big American cars, but first she had to rise through the ranks. Her first rally at the wheel – in a small NSU – was the Criterium des Cévennes in a blizzard, where she won the Ladies' Cup, plus the wheel of a works car. This was the start of a career that encompassed 14 successful years of racing!

In the Routes du Nord, the NSU mechanic – in order to save on weight – had removed the heating; they all but froze …!

Very sporty, Marie-Claude skied, skated, rode horses and played tennis. She was – and is – highly spontaneous and tenacious, with a very positive outlook. (Greder was to nickname her 'never satisfied.') Thanks to that combination, and with the will and desire to be a champion in her own right, she became the equal of the best male racing drivers. As with Annie Soisbault, her target was not the Ladies' Cup but the 'winning.'

In 1969, Marie-Claude was part of the famous Greder Racing team and made a name for herself in European rallies with large Opel Commodores and Camaros, taking the French championship title to start off with, until 1972, when she even clinched the European title. Winning the Tour de Corse, the Tours Autos, and the Monte Carlo, she was the best of the French women.

But Marie-Claude insisted on retaining her femininity: "I'm a woman like any other," who liked window-shopping and didn't turn up her nose at dresses and perfumes. Being an object of curiosity was often uncomfortable, but not as serious as skidding on a sheet of black ice!

Marie-Claude Beaumont during the 1969 Monte Carlo. (JFB Collection)

Marie-Claude Beaumont. She began rallying with Claudine Trautmann in a Lancia in the 1965 Monte Carlo. (M Louche Collection)

1967 Monte Carlo, and first attempts with the NSU team. Marie-Claude was still learning, but soon began winning. (M Louche Collection)

Right: Marie-Claude moved to Team Greder, with large Opel Commodores at Monte Carlo, in 1969. She finished second of the ladies and 15th overall. (JFB Collection)

Far right: Victory at the 1971 Tour Auto in a Camaro Z28, with Martine de La Grandrive. They were the first of the ladies. (M Louche Collection)

1971 Tour Auto: victory in close-up. (JFB Collection)

A good sport, Marie-Claude rescued two direct competitors who were balanced precariously over a precipice in the Alpine Cup. With Henri Greder, she lost the hard top of her Corvette at over 200km/h (124mph) during the Paris Mille Kilomètres – which just missed Jean Sage's Porsche Kremer 911S! She also took part in the Targa Florio where the Italian reception for this ravishing blonde driver was more than warm, but she managed not to lose her head.

Ladies' Cup at the 1971 RAC Rally. (JFB Collection)

New beginnings at Le Mans. For the first time in twenty years, a woman, at last. Marie-Claude Beaumont and Henri Greder take turns in their Corvette at the 1971 Le Mans. They had to later withdraw with engine failure. (JFB Collection)

Le Mans 1972. President Pompidou, De Adamich (Alfa), Van Lennep (Scudria Suisse) and Marie-Claude Beaumont. (JFB Collection)

Le Mans 1973. Christine Beckers, Gérard Larrousse and Marie-Claude Beaumont, with a Greder Chevrolet Corvette. (JFB Collection)

Le Mans. Marie-Claude's BMW 635 has had a collision. Time to withdraw. (JFB Collection)

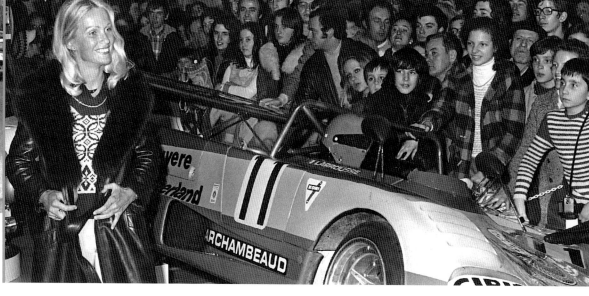

Above right: 1973 Salon de Paris. Marie-Claude in front of the Lola Archambeaud-T290 BMW Schnitzer managed by Jean Sage. (JFB Collection)

Team Aseptogyl, scantily clad, in tights: Dacremont, Trautmann, Palayer and Hoepfner. (Neyret Collection)

In 1971, Marie-Claude made her first appearance at Le Mans, continuing to take part until 1976 with Chevrolet, Alpine and Porsche. "Woman to compete in the Le Mans 24-Hours," was the tabloid headline. "I would happily have foregone such a claim to fame, and seeing my name and my photo on the front page alongside an amorous diva didn't particularly send me into raptures …" she said.

That a woman should enter Le Mans caused quite a stir at the time, as, ever since Annie Bousquet's accident at Rheims, the sporting authorities were wary of women in very fast cars. In 1954, Gilberte Thirion had been evicted from the track at the last minute after the qualifying heats. Macho images lived on: "the directors of the ACO received a petition from La Baule, where the signatory, in the name of 21 people, rose up against one woman competitor: 'In this man's race, we don't want skirts,' ranted the protester. We can assure the sports-lovers of La Baule that Marie-Claude Beaumont will not be wearing a skirt while at the wheel of the powerful Chevrolet Corvette." *L'Équipe*, 9 June 1971.

Unfortunately, the engine broke down, handing victory to the Porsche 917s. Marie-Claude returned to Le Mans five times, but, in 1974, turned to track championships and came second behind Henri Greder. Under the management of Gérard Larrousse, she was also to drive in several heats in the world track championship, in an Alpine A441 with Lella Lombardi (one of the five women in F1), against the greatest: Pescarolo, Laffitte and Jabouille.

In 1977, she hung up her helmet to devote herself to press relations in F1. A hard choice, as she no longer drove though was a part of the Renault F1 scene.

Nowadays, Marie-Claude lives in Lausanne, and, as a photographer, continues to follow the F1 circus.

The Team Aseptogyl

In 1971, Bob Neyret was a dentist as well as an astute businessman. In order to promote his brand new toothpaste in the hypermarkets, he hit on the idea of using his weekend obsession; selling to those hypermarkets an advertising concept based on motor racing, dressed up with a touch of glamour in the form of beautiful female racing drivers. These young women had to be carefully selected, as beauty alone was not enough; they also had to be able to produce results. Only winners hit the front page!

Bob – who had driven in rallies in the Citroën team since the 1960s, having begun in the Mont-Blanc with Galtier in a 4CV in 1955 – organized a ruthless selection process, in live conditions, in the special stage of the Chartreuse rally. The girls would be driving small new Group 3 Alpine saloon cars that Jean Rédélé – a skiing friend from Megève who was delighted by the idea of using the female team to promote his marque – undertook to maintain for Bob throughout the season.

The media impact was enormous and the magazine *L'Équipe* presented this bright pink stable on its front page (those small saloon cars were painted in red, white and strawberry pink). Amongst them was Claudine Trautmann, champion of France (she was later to become manager of Team Autogyl); Marie-Odile Desvignes, a former employee of Europcar and fashion model (particularly pretty, she earnt the status of racing driver during the 1971 season); Annick Girard, the most talented; Marie-Dominique Guichard, wife to the son of St Etienne Casino's Managing Director (crafty Mr Neyret! for the sponsors); Marie-Pierre Palayer; Françoise Concori, a young girl from Grenoble (and Michèle Mouton's future co-driver); Christine Rouff, a dentist in Grenoble; Marie Laurent, a Chrysler Barracuda driver;

Team Aseptogyl in 1971, with its new collection of female Alpine drivers. (Neyret Collection)

Christine Dacremont drove for Aseptogyl in the 1972 Tour Auto, but she had fallen off a motorbike, and had to take her crutches. (JFB Collection)

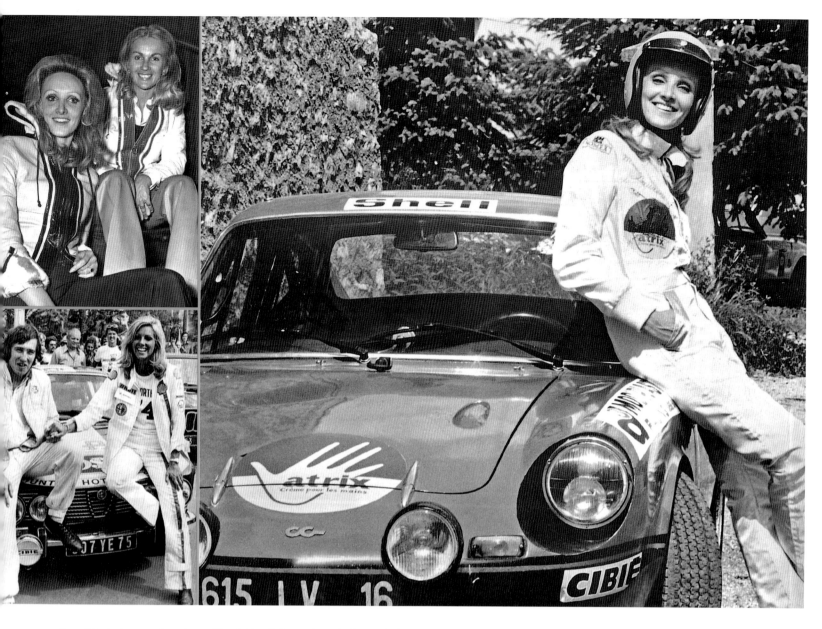

Charlotte Julien, sister-in-law of the wife of Claude Laurent, the great Daf driver, and, later on in 1973, even Pat Moss!

1971 proved a significant year as these racing drivers claimed many Ladies' Cups. They returned in 1972, adding Marianne Hoepfner, the recent champion of France (usurped by Marie-Claude Beaumont), Christine Dacremont from the Ardennes, and 1971 champion of France, Corinne Koppenhague and the Belgian Christine Beckers, plus a co-driver, Yveline Vanon, who became one of the pillars of the stable. The success of the French 1972 season was exemplified by an Aseptogyl one-two-three in the Paris-Saint-Raphaël.

In 1973, the concept of a female team was working so well that it increased number, with Peugeot entering 504s in African rallies. With the addition of Anne-Charlotte Verney, the team did the 3-vehicle Sahara Rally Raid (alone, without help), and, whilst at

it, the Bandama Rally with the same 504. They were seventh and eighth. The team also took part in the 1975 Morocco Rally, winning the Ladies' Cup. Bob Neyret reinvested in his increasingly competitive cars and gave his 'Pink Panthers' (he was to come under attack from Disney for this term, found nevertheless all over the press …) the Lancia Stratos and the new Alpine A310. And then there were the pretty little Autobianchi A112s with the Chardonnet network, and a huge success at the Monte Carlo.

Public relations operations at the Le Mans 24-Hours provided an interlude that was keenly noted by the French rugby team. Marianne Hoepfner drove there with Lella Lombardi in 1976. Promotion in Italy was based around Fiats (Anna Cambiaghi, Maurizia Baresi, Antonella Mandelli and Christina Bertone) in 1978. Another promotion at the Brazil Rally had Fiat 147s and ecological fuel based on sugar cane. Bob Neyret took with him three European champions, Hoepfner, Cambiaghi and Baresi, who won their class.

The same idea was used in Europe, with female drivers in the Alfa 1500 TI selected from the Alfa Romeo network. This was a huge success until the 1980s, when girls also went to the Paris-Dakar with 260hp Unic lorries. That year, Bob Neyret sold the Aseptogyl brand, but not the team, which continued until the 1990s!

1975 Tour Auto. Anne-Charlotte Verney and Miss Fouquet getting ready during the technical checks of their Porsche 911. (JFB Collection)

The Aseptogyl Pink Panthers in the 1973 Monte Carlo in Alpine Groupe 4s: Marie-Odile Desvignes and Dacremont; Pat Moss and Crelin; and Hoepfner and Vanoni. (Neyret Collection)

Above & left: Operation Sahara Rally Raid and the 1973 Bandama Rally for Peugeot. Two teams were to set off from Paris, crossing the Sahara and Africa, to take the start of the Bandama Rally in Abidjan: Verney, Hoepfner, Palayer, Vanoni, Trautmann and Dacremont. They returned to France by road. (Neyret Collection)

Morocco Rally with Peugeot for Desvignes, Trautmann and Hoepfner in 1975. (Neyret Collection)

Dacremont and Galli. Ladies' Cup at the 1977 Monte Carlo and 1976 European championship for Dacremont and her Stratos. (M Louche Collection)

Team Aseptogyl mounts a PR campaign during the 1976 Le Mans, with the French rugby team. Spanghero, Boutier, Anne-Charlotte Verney, Marianne Hoepfner, Christine Dacremont, Marie Pierre Palayer and Françoise Conconi. (Neyret Collection)

Above & left: Operation A112 Abarth for the Chardonnet network. Monte Carlo 1976. Joël Chardin, Biche, Marianne Hoepfner, D Denard, Christine Dacremont, Marie Dominique Cousin, an unknown, Corinne Copenhague-Tarnaud and Marie-Odile Desvignes. (Neyret Collection)

155

1976 Le Mans with Lella Lombardi and Christine Dacremont in a long-chassis Lancia Stratos. First of the ladies, 20th overall. (Neyret Collection)

Operation Aseptogyl Citroën Diesel CX, Monte Carlo 1978. Dacremont, Hoepfner and Oksala. With Marlène Cotton, Citroën competition manager. (Neyret Collection)

1978 Tour de Corse for Aseptogyl and Fiat. Anna Cambiaghi, Erica Marengi, Maurizia Baresi, Iva Boggio, Antonelle Mandelli and Christina Bertone. (Neyret Collection)

Marianne Hoepfner in a hillclimb with an Alpine F2. (Neyret Collection)

Team Aseptogyl at the Paris-Dakar in 1980 with a 260hp Iveco Unic 4x4. Hoepfner, Baresi, Cambiaghi, Perrier, Anderson and Palayer: the Pink Panthers. (Neyret Collection)

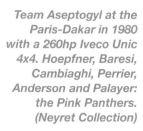

Operation Brazil. Ethanol fuel, based on sugar cane. Baresi, Hoepfner and Cambiaghi with their Fiat 147. (Neyret Collection)

Corinne Koppenhague (1947-)

"With her glasses still perched on the end of her nose, giving the false impression of a country schoolmistress, it's the petite youngster who goes up," was the headline of *L'Automobile* magazine in 1970. She had won the French national female rally of the year title with her Porsche 911 (and Marie-Claude Beaumont had won the rally championship in a Camaro).

Corinne was a petite Parisian who lived between the Lycée Molière and La Muette, but nevertheless already had motoring connections. Her cousin was Marie-Claire Cibié and her mother had been an ambulance driver in 1940, though it was more her association with young scoundrels like Jean-Pierre Jabouille, Jacques Laffite, Guy Ligier, Sylvain Garant and Georges Houel senior (him again!), in the Le Koala café in the Place Dauphine that inspired her to take up competition.

In 1969, a trip to the Rheims 12-Hours, where she was looking after the pit for Garant (who was racing with Jacques Frey in a Ferrari), finally clinched it for her – she went home smitten.

She began as team-mate to Marie-Pierre Palayer and Bob Wollek at the Cévennes, and Thierry Sabine in a Porsche 911 at the AGACI 300. In the end, Rey lent her a 911 for the Tour Auto. She entered the 1970 championship and won!

On the 1971 Tour de France, she was with Christine Rouff in a Porsche 911. Their mascot was called 'On a diet,' and slept in the glove compartment for the entire rally: she was a tortoise! During any technical assistance, the mechanics fed her on fresh lettuce leaves. In 1974 it was the Monte Carlo in an Aseptogyl Autobianchi A112, then it was driving an Alfa 2000 and the French championships in Group 1, then the Ronde Cévenole, the Vercors Vivarais Rally, etc. When racing with Christine Dacremont, their Opel Kadette lost a wheel and ended up in a field. "We were covered in mud. We looked like wild boar!"

In 1975, Corinne took part in the Le Mans 24-Hours in a Porsche 911, with Anne-Charlotte Verney and Yvette Fontaine, coming 11th in the scratch and second of the GTs – no problem at all. She also took part in a Volvo Cup in Sweden. "It's very tough. Compared to the R5 Cup these are child's play!" In 1976, life was hard for a privateer wanting to succeed. She prepared an Alfa Sud that she attached to the rear of her Volvo and departed for the European Cup that François Landon had organized.

In 1977, she steered her career towards motorcycles and set off with Thierry Sabine to do the Croisière Verte race. This was also the first motorcycle Paris-Dakar; the second would be completed in a Willis

Jeep, bought for 20,000 francs and sponsored by CB Midland. "We were always running out of petrol, until we realised that our fuel pipe was too short and didn't go down to the bottom of the tank for the last twenty litres!" Corinne had found her calling. She did ten Dakar rallies, which included driving in a Range Rover with the Halt Up Garage. She once overturned in a Toyota after losing a wheel, returning from Tamanrasset directly to hospital in Paris. These days, Corinne lives near Chamonix, in the Savoie. She divides her life between her dog, her small chalet, her motocross bike – and skiing in the winter, of course!

Corinne Koppenhague in a Porsche 911, helmeted to the eyes. (Koppenhague Collection)

Corinne in a Volvo coupé. (Koppenhague Collection)

Corinne Koppenhague and her 911 at the 1970 Grand National. Ladies' Cup. (M Louche Collection)

Corinne at the 1972 Monte Carlo in an Alpine with Dacremont. The rally stopped there. (M Louche Collection)

Michèle Mouton (1951-)

Never has a female racing driver got as far and been as successful as her male counterpart. Being female rally champion of France six times (1974, 1975 and 1977-1980) is okay; being female champion of Europe five times (1974, 1975, 1977, 1978 and 1982) is even better. But Michèle Mouton's goal was to go all the way: to be world champion, and she came close to this in 1982 with second place, thanks to her Audi Quattro. Vice-champion of the world!

At the age of 20, this attractive girl from Grasse still didn't know what a rally was, and got into motor racing by accident whilst doing a gymkhana with a Renault 4L. Then, as so often happens, a friend took her along as navigator in the 1973 Monte Carlo in a Peugeot 304. Seeing her enthusiasm, her father gave her a season to try herself out with a Renault Alpine. It went like a dream and the rest is history. Michèle raced Alpines for four years, then an A112 and Porsche 911s, followed by a Lancia Stratos and Fiat 131 Abarths for three years. She spent three years with Audi and the legendary Quattro, and ended her racing career on a brilliant note in group B at Peugeot with the 205 Turbo 16. Her life story could fill a book. As Camille du Gast, Elisabeth Junek, Pat Moss and Annie Soisbault had done before her, she had a profound effect on a century of racing ...

Michèle Mouton. The Alpine era. (M Louche Collection)

Michèle Mouton at the 1977 Monte Carlo, in a Chardonnet Autobianchi Abarth. (Blanchet Collection)

Michèle Mouton and Françoise Conconi at the 1978 Tour Auto, in a Fiat 131 Abarth. In spite of those glum looks, the Ladies' Cup was theirs. (M Louche Collection)

Far left: Michèle Mouton on the attack in an Audi Quattro at the 1982 Monte Carlo. This was the year to achieve the world championchip title! (M Louche Collection)

1977 Monte Carlo Rally. At the same time as Michèle Mouton, Philippe Douste-Blazy, still a doctor here before becoming a politician, a novice in an Opel Kadett GTE. Our 'politicians' did like their cars. (M Louche Collection)

Michèle Mouton in a Peugeot 205 Turbo 16. (JFB Collection)

7

Bernie Eccleston, chief executive of F1 and father of two daughters, nevertheless claimed, during an interview, that he doubted whether a woman could ever achieve pre-eminence in this sport, taking into account the problems of sponsors, financial support, and a female racing driver's credibility. However, with dear Bernie's business instinct ever on the lookout for a scoop, he hastened to add that his "greatest wish would be to find a real gem; for example, a Spanish-speaking black girl, preferably Jewish or Moslem ..." Which only goes to prove that there have certainly been one or two flamboyant characters over the years!

F1

Maria Teresa's Maserati at the 1958 Belgian Grand Prix. (JFB Collection)

Five women in F1

Yes, F1 is one of the most physically demanding motorsport disciplines. And, no, it was not only made for men, even if Henry Ford felt that women would be unable to withstand as much 'G' force as their male counterparts. For this championship, which was created in 1950, there have, nevertheless, been few attempts from women. However, throughout the history of F1, five women were to carve a name for themselves: Maria Teresa de Filippis in 1958, Lella Lombardi in 1975, Divina Galica in 1976, Desiré Wilson in 1980, and Giovanna Amati in 1992.

Maria Teresa de Filippis, from Italy, was the first woman in F1. She drove in three Grands Prix with a Maserati 250F in 1958, and her best result was a second place at Spa in the Belgian GP. She almost qualified in a Porsche F2 in the 1959 Monaco Grand Prix, but withdrew on learning of the death of her mentor, Jean Behra, who was killed on the Avus track at the German GP.

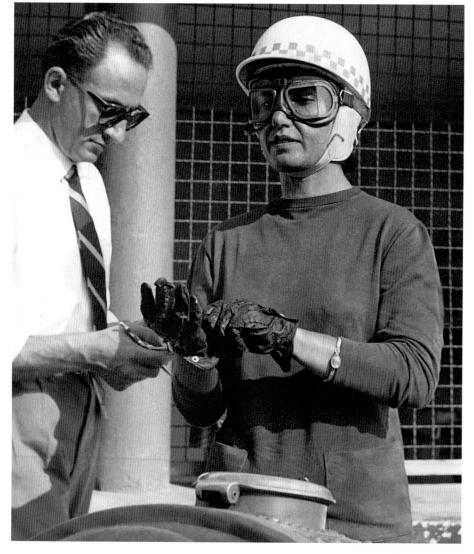

Maria Teresa de Filippis – the first woman in F1 – at the 1958 Monza Grand Prix. (JFB Collection)

Lella Lombardi, also from Italy, qualified 10 times in 14 Grands Prix events, finishing in the first six at the Spanish Grand Prix with the March stable, and thus gained the only ½ point of all the women drivers in the history of F1 to this day. She continued her racing career at the Eurotourisme circuit in Alfa GTV6s and Ford Sierras. The 'Tigress of Turin' was also the team manager of her own organization, Lella Lombardi Autosport, when, worn out after a long illness, she died on 3 March 1992. She had raced several times in the Le Mans 24-Hours event and in Nascar in the USA.

Divina Galica, British Olympic ski champion, failed to qualify for the 1976 British Grand Prix in a Surtees-Ford. She was also unsuccessful at the Argentine and 1978 Brazil Grands Prix with the Hesketh stable.

Desiré Wilson, from South Africa, also failed to qualify in a Williams for the 1980 British Grand Prix.

Giovanna Amati, again from Italy, was the daughter of a wealthy industrialist (she was kidnapped by the Red Brigade!), and had been mad about motorsport since her childhood. She owned a 500cc Honda motorbike, which she secretly rode around Rome by night, without a licence.

A childhood friend, Elio de Angelis, gave her driving lessons, and she soon progressed to the Italian F3 championships. "I had to frequently change the decoration of my car so that the other boys couldn't identify me from one race to the next. For some of them, it was frankly intolerable to be overtaken by a girl and they often deliberately opted for a collision rather than lose a place." She has a strong personality, and is alleged to have had romances with Nicki Lauda and Flavio Briatore, whilst he was managing director of Team Benetton.

She signed up for the 1992 season with Brabham, but there, too, failed to qualify in three Grands Prix events. She continued her career in a category of racing called Sport Proto. Nowadays, she is a journalist for the press, as well as for Italian television.

Let's hope that the list doesn't stop there, though old prejudices die hard ...

Desiré Wilson in F1.
(JFB Collection)

Lella Lombardi in Formula 3. The second woman in F1. (JFB Collection)

Divina Gallica in F1. (Getty Images)

Giovanna Amati in F1. (DR)

from 1900 to the 1970s

This is a non-exhaustive list of all the female racing drivers that I encountered during research for this book. They are arranged in alphabetical order, along with some of the sporting events and the cars in which they raced, in order to make it easier to place them in time and historical context. A timely phenomenon of liberty in their day, female racing drivers are more numerous today. As time advances, the harder it becomes to list them all. So, 'forgotten ladies,' please don't bear a grudge if you don't find yourself in this list. That will come in another book!

ACHARD-DESOCHE Paulette	St Raphaël '54 – 203 Peugeot
AGOSTINI (F)	Tour de Course '74 – Ascona; '76 – Porsche Carrera
AITKEN-WALKER Louise (GB)	Champion des Rallyes '82; Monte Carlo '83 – Alfasud TI, WRC 90
ALBRIZZI Contessa Elsa	Course Padoue-Padoue 1899 – Benz
ALDER-SMITH (GB)	Liège-Rome-Liège '63 – Mini Cooper
ALEXANDER (GB)	Monte Carlo '27 – Steyr
ALEY Jean (Mlle Curtis) (GB)	Brighton '58 – Mini Cooper; Nürburgring 6-Hours '62 – Mini Cooper; Snetterton '62
ALLAN Margaret (GB)	Monte Carlo '34 – Triumph; '35 – AC; Le Mans '35 – MG, Triumph, AC; Coupe des Alpes
ALLARD Eleanor (GB)	Brighton '47-'49; Monte Carlo '50-'52 – Allard; St Raphaël '51
ALLEN Dorothy (GB)	Brooklands '32 – Lagonda
ALTHAM P	Shelsley-Walsh '33 – Bentley
ALZIARI de ROQUEFORT Lucienne (F)	Rallye Allier '54 – Panhard; Liège-Rome-Liège '55 – Panhard; St Raphaël '54 – Panhard
AMATI Giovana (I)	Le Mans '92 – Judd (F1); Kyalami Brabham '92
ANDERSON (GB)	Monte Carlo '35 – Riley
ANDERSON Janet (USA)	Race '58 USA
ANDRINA (F)	Tour de France '84 – Visa Chrono
ANGELVIN (F)	Monte Carlo '50-'51 – Simca 8
APPLEYARD Pat (GB) (daughter of Sir Lyons)	London Rallye '51 – XK120; Morecomb Rallye '52
ARCHAMBAUD Françoise (F)	Monte Carlo '58; Tour de France '58 – Alfa Giulietta; Coupe USA '59 – Alfa Giulietta TI; Liège-Rome-Liège '61 – ID 19
ARCHE Anna	Spain '99
ASHFIELD Laura (GB)	Monte Carlo '53 – Sunbeam; '55 – Zéphir; '56 – Standard-Vanguard; Rallye Tulipes '56
ASTBURY Jackie (GB)	Monte Carlo '35-'36; Mille Miles RAC Rallye '35 – Singer
ATWOOD Margaret (GB)	USA '09 Maxwell
AUMAS (F)	Tour de Course '58-'59 – Giulietta; Tour de France '59 – Alfa Giulietta
AVANZO Maria Antonietta, baronne d' (I)	Speed Week in Brescia '21 – Alfa Romeo; Rocca di Papa '27 – Maserati; Coppa Galenga '28 –Maserati; Mille Miles '28 – Chrysler 72; '29 – Alfa 6C 1750; '31 – Bugatti 43; '32 – Alfa 1750
AVERSTEDT Viveca (S)	Sweden '97
AXELSEN JOHNSEN (S)	Monte Carlo '49 – Ford V8
AYLMER Mimy (I)	Mille Miles '29 – Lancia Lambda; '35 – Fiat 508
BAGARRY (F)	Monte Carlo '53 – 4CV; '55 – 203; St Raphaël '54 – 4CV Renault
BAHR Lotte (D)	Monte Carlo '30 – Steyr; Liège-Rome-Liège '34 – Adler; '38 – Imperia; 39 Adler
BAL Georgette	St Raphaël '54
BALACHINSKY	St Raphaël '54
BANCONS (F)	Rallye St Jean de Luz '54 – Simca
BARBIER (F)	Tour de France '14 – Zedel
BARESI Mauricia (I)	Tour de Corse '78 – Fiat 127; Monte Carlo '83 – Alfasud 1500 TI
BARON (F)	Tour de Corse '66 – Alfa GTA
BAROZZI Maria (I)	Italy '56
BASHFORD-MALKIE Helen (GB)	'85 – Toyota F3, F1, FF2000, GT Supersport; '97 – Daytona, Historic 2002 – Lotus 23B
BAVEREY Anne	Monte Carlo '83 – Alfasud TI; Champion of France, Mountains '82
BAXTER Prudence (USA)	USA '50
BAYER Sonja (D)	Germany 2000

BAYROU (F)	Rallye St Jean de Luz '54 – Panhard
BEAULIEU (de) Marie-Claire (Mlle Cibié) (F)	Tour de France '54 – Porsche 550
BEAUMONT Marie-Claude (Mlle Charmasson) (F)	Cévennes '65 – NSU; Monte Carlo '66 – Lancia; '67 – NSU; '69-'70 – Commodore; '71-'72 – Ascona; Tour de Corse '66, '68 – NSU; '69, '73 – Opel; 1000km Paris '70 – Corvette; Tour de France '69, '71, '72, '73 – Camaro; Monte Carlo '71 – Comodore GSE; Le Mans '71, '76 – Corvette Alpine A441
BECKERS Christine (B)	Rallye Tulipes '68; Spa '67-'68; Rallye Cévennes – GTA; Formule V-VW; Tour de Corse '77 – Celica; Le Mans '76/'77 – Chevron & Inaltera; Spa '75 – Triumph Dolomite
BENZ Bertha	Pforzheim 1888
BERNARDI Daphné (I)	Italy '53
BERNIS (F)	Tour de France '54 – 4CV 1063
BERTAPELLE Patricia (F)	Tour de France '85 – 205 GTI
BERTONE Christine (I)	Tour de Corse '78 – Fiat 127
BIGNARDI Isabella	Monte Carlo '83 – AlfasudTI
BIRREL Jennifer (GB)	GB '71
BIZERAY (F)	Bol d'Or '54 – 4CV spéciale
BIZZARI (F)	Tour de Corse '79 – Audi
BLACKLEY Sherry (GB)	GB '71
BLANCHOUD Mado (F)	Monte Carlo '54 – 356; '58 – Alfa Giulietta; '61 – Saab; '62 – Anglia; Tour de France '56 – Saab; '58 – 356
BLANKSTONE Margareth	Shelsley-Walsh '78 – Twincam U2
BOER WASSENAAR (de)	Monte Carlo '30 – Steyr
BOESWILLWALD	Tour de France '51; Monte Carlo '51 – 203
BOGGIO Iva (I)	Tour de Corse '78 – Fiat127
BOND Miss	Brooklands '28 – Bugatti
BORREL (F)	Rallye Perche '54
BOSSY	St Raphaël '54
BOSTON Mrs	Coupe des Alpes '14 – Cadillac
BOUCHER (F)	Tour de France '51 – Simca Sp.; Monte Carlo '51 – Simca 8
BOUCHET Claudine (Mme Vanson, Mme Trautmann) (F)	Liège-Rome-Liège '62/'63 – DS19; '66 – Lancia; Monte Carlo '63/'64 – ID19; Tour de Corse '58 – Simca; '60, '63 – DS
BOUDIN (F)	GP Marseille '27
BOURBON de (F)	Monte Carlo '39 – Simca
BOURDENEAU (F)	Bol d'Or
BOUSCIOL (F)	Rallye AGACI '64 – TR4
BOUSQUET Annie (Mlle Schaeffer) (A)	Monte Carlo '53 – 4CV; GP Agen '53 – D Bracer; Rallye Perla San Remo '53; Rallye Dauphiné '53 – 4CV; Spa '53 – Fiat 1100; Tour de France '54 – 4CV; Mille Miles '53 – 4CV; '54 – Gordini; 12H Hyères; Monte Carlo '55 – Panhard Dyna; 24H Paris '55; GP Agadir '55 – Porsche; GP Dakar; Record heure Montlhéry '55 – Porsche; '56 – TR2; 1000km Paris '56 – Maserati 1500; 12H Reims '56 – Porsche 550 spider
BOVE	Liège-Rome-Liège '32 – FN
BRACCIALINI Corinna (I)	Mille Miles '30 – Alfa 1500
BRANFORD	St Raphaël '54
BRENGLE Nadine	USA '61
BROWN Daena (GB)	GB '30
BRUCE Mildred (Mrs Victor Bruce) (GB)	Monte Carlo '27/'28 – AC; '30 – Hillman; Raid Artic; Record Montlhéry '27 – AC; Record Montlhéry '29 – Bentley; Brooklands – AC; records aériens multiples
BRUNNEL Kitty (GB)	Shelsley-Walsh '33 – Bugatti; Monte Carlo '28/'29/'30 – Talbot; Hastings Rallye '34 – AC
BRUSSEL	Monte Carlo '36 – Ford
BRYNER Lilian (USA)	Le Mans '93, '94, '95, '97 – Porsche 911; Porsche Cup; 24H Daytona '96; 1000km Monza '98; Sebring '98 – Ferrari 333; Spa 2000
BUCKNELL G. and D. (GB)	Barnet Trial '30
BUCQUET (F)	Tour de France '33 – Amilcar
BUNSELMEYER (USA)	USA '50
BURNETT (GB)	Brooklands '29 – Alvis RIGGS
BURT Patsy (GB)	Shelsley-Walsh '57 – Cooper; RAC '54 – XK120; '59 – Anglia; Brighton Speed '56 – Connaught F1; '68; 1000km Nürburgring '57 – MGA
BUSSET (F)	St Raphaël '54
CABIEU-PARRAN Mlle. (F)	Monte Carlo '12 – Lion Peugeot
CAFFIRI	Rallye Amazon '66 – DS19
CALI Cathy (F)	Paris-Dakar; Rally Cross

CAMBIAGHI Anna (I)	Le Mans '77 – Osella; Tour de Corse '77, '78 – Fiat, Celica; Monte Carlo '79 – CX GTI; Rallye Brasil '79 – Fiat 147
CANCRE Michèle (Mme d'Orgeix) (F)	Team d'A. Soisbault (Stock car)
CARDWELL Lucille	Kenya '59-'60 – Porsche RS; East African Track '60, '62 – Porsche Spyder; East African Safari '61 – Zephyr
CAREY de BONY (F)	Monte Carlo '54 – 4CV
CARLISLE Christabel (Lady Watson) (GB)	Brandshatch '61, '62 – Mini; Silverstone, Goodwood, Crystal Palace, 6H Nürburgring, Roskilde '62, '63; Monte Carlo '62 – MG; Monte Carlo '63 – Austin-Healey; Sebring '63
CARTLAND Barbara (GB)	'31 (Brooklands race organiser)
CAZON (F)	St Raphaël '54 – Panhard
CELLIER de BURIANE (F)	Monte Carlo '30 – Peugeot
CHALENCON (de) (F)	Tour de Corse '62 – ID 19
CHAMPNEY Dorothy (GB)	Le Mans '34 – Riley
CHARDIN (F)	Tour de France '73 – 911S; Tour de Corse '78 – Fiat127
CHARLOTTE (F)	Tour de Corse '74 – A110
CHARRIERE (F)	Champion of France '70 – R8 Gordini
CHASLERIE-REY (F)	St Raphaël '54
CHERRET (F)	Monte Carlo '56 – 403; '58 – Aronde; Liège-Rome-Liège '57 – Simca; Tour de Corse '57 – Aronde
CHESTER Ann (USA)	US '50
CHETWIND Joan (GB)	Brooklands '29 record – Meadows-Lea Francis; Le Mans '31; Monte Carlo '30 – Lea Francis; Le Mans '31 – MG
CHEVALLEY Nadine (F)	Tour de France '69 – BMW 1600 TI
CHIESA (Comtessa della) (I)	St Raphaël '53 – Lancia Aurelia
CHILTON Doris (GB)	Shelsley-Walsh '22 – Arrol Johnston
CHITWOOD Joie (USA)	US '67
CHOLLAT (F)	St Raphaël '54
CHRISTINE (Beckers) (B)	Spa '67 – NSU; '68 – Alfa 1750; '72 – Alfa GTV; '73 – Opel Commodore; Le Mans '74 – Chevron B23; '76, '77 – Inaltera
CLARKE Françoise (F)	Monte Carlo 554 – Sunbeam-Talbot
CLARKE Joanna (GB)	GB 2002
COLONA Princess Fernanda Dorina (I)	Mille Miles '30 – Alfa 1750
COMIRATO Lia (Mme Alberto) Dumas-Comirato (I)	Mille Miles '37 – Fiat 508; '48 – Fiat 1100 Sport; '47
CONCONI Françoise (F)	Team M Mouton
CONRAD Kitty (GB)	New Market race track – New Jersey '33
CONVERT Yolande (F)	St Raphaël '54 – 4CV
COOKE Joy (GB)	Shelsley-Walsh '50 – Kieft; Monte Carlo '51 – Standard-Vanguard; Monte Carlo '56 – Ford Zéphir; Rallye Tulipes '51 – Standard
COOPER (GB)	Monte Carlo '62 – Sunbeam-Alpine
CORDERY Violette (Mrs Hindmarsh) (GB)	Brooklands '25 – Invicta; 10 Miles Record Monza '26
CORDESSE (F)	Tour de Corse '74-'76 – A110; '78 – Kadett
CORNELIUS SYBRANDY	Monte Carlo '36, '38 – DKW
CORTANZE (de) Fernande (Mlle Hustinx) (F)	Monte Carlo '51-'54; Tour de France '54 – 203; St Raphaël '54 – Peugeot 203
CORTANZE (de) Martine (de la Grandrive) (F)	Paris-Dakar
COTTON (F)	Monte Carlo '35 – MG; '36 – Aston; Monte Carlo '37 – Hillman; '38 – Lancia
COUZY Madeleine (F)	Tour de France '64
COWELL Roberta (ex-Robert Cowell) (GB)	Shelsley-Walsh '39 – Alta; '57 – Emryson-Alta
CRISTIAN Sara (USA)	USA '49
CULLEN	Monte Carlo '56 – Austin A40
CUMMINGS Ivy (GB)	Brooklands '25 – GN, Bugatti (Black Bess)
CUNEO Joan Newton (USA)	USA Glidden Tour '05; New Orleans '09
CUNLIFFE May (GB)	Shelsley-Walsh '26 – Bentley 3 l; '28 – GP Sunbeam; South Port Sands '28 – Sunbeam; Shelsley '36 – Alta
DACREMONT Christine (F)	Monte Carlo '72 – Alpine; Tour de Corse '78 – Fiat 127; Le Mans '75-'78 – Stratos and WM
DARBISHIRE Sheila (GB)	Douglas IOM '47 – ERA-Riley; Prescott
DARRE-BRANDT	Monte Carlo '34, '35 – Chrysler
DASSONVILLE (F)	Rallye Yonne '54 – 2CV
DAVIS Mary (USA)	USA '55
DEARBORN Gloria (USA)	USA '57
DEBRA	Liège-Rome-Liège '65 – Porsche

DELL Jenny (GB)	Goodwin Trophy '69 – Diva; RAC Champ '70 – Costin-Nathan
DELORME Marguerite	St Raphaël '53, '54 – Simca Vedette
DEMAI (F)	Tour de France '70 – Capri
DENTON Jean (Baronne of Wakefield) (GB)	Mini, Morgan, F3 London-Sidney '69 – MGB; Mexico '70 – Morris 1800
DERANCOURT Albertine (F)	GP Lyon '29 – Bugatti
DESCOLAS Claire (F)	Record Yacco, Montlhéry '37; Coupe des Alpes '30-'39 – Lancia and Bugatti; '47-'48 – Aprilia
DESPREZ Marie (F)	Le Mans '33 – Bugatti 54
DESVIGNES Marie-Odile (F)	Tour de France '72 – Alpine
DEUTSCH de la MEURTHE (Mme) (F)	St Raphaël '30 – Hispano 46 CV Binder
DINSDALE (GB)	Monte Carlo '30 – Vauxhall
DOBSON M J (GB)	Mille Miles Rallye '36 – MG
DOMLEO Val (Mrs Morley) (GB)	Monte Carlo '61 – Ford, Mini, TR3 Tulip; RAC; Alpine Rallye
DON Kaye (GB)	Brooklands Record '32 – Sunbeam
DON Rita (GB)	Brooklands '33 – Riley, Bugatti
DORE (F)	Monte Carlo '30 – Chenard and Walker
DORNIER (F)	Monte Carlo '28 – Mathis
DROLET Smokey (USA)	Daytona '59
DUBONNET Lorraine (F)	Rallyes '50
DUBOSC Michèle (F)	Rallye Sestrières '59 – TR3. Navigatrice d'A. Soisbault, Rosinski, etc.
DUBUC-TAINE (F)	St Raphaël '34 – Hotchkiss
DUNHAM (GB)	Monte Carlo '53, '54 – Rover 75
DUNOD Milka	Le Mans 2001 – Judd; 2002 – Panoz
DYKES (Mrs Bill Urquhart) (GB)	Brooklands '28 – Alvis
EATON Collen (Mrs Hugh) (GB)	Le Mans '35 – MG
ECCLES Marjorie (Ray) (Mrs Lindsay) (GB)	Le Mans '37 – Singer; Brooklands '36 – Rapier; Crystal Palace '37 – Rapier; Shelsley-Walsh – Lagonda Rapier
EDENNING Inga Lill (S)	Sweden '63
EHRINGE	Monte Carlo '64 – VW 1500; Liège-Rome-Liège '64 – VW
EINSIEDEL Comtesse Margot	Targa Florio '28 – Bugatti
ELDER Viviane (F)	Le Mans '49 – Simca 8 Tank
ELLIS Christabel (GB)	Brooklands '08 – GCG
ELLISON Eileen (GB)	Rallye RAC '32 – Bugatti; RAC '35 – Lagonda; Brooklands '32 – Bugatti; South African GP '36 – Lagonda, Maserati; Klausen Renennen; GP Albi
ENGEMAN Lian (D)	12H Sebring '67; Crystal Palace '69 – Anglia; Spa '70 – Alfa 2 l; German Champion '72 – Capri
EVANS de LOPEZ (Mx)	Carrera Panama '54 – Porsche 356
EVANS Doreen (GB)	Shelsley-Walsh '35 – MG R; Le Mans '35 – MG; Brooklands '36 – MG
FACETTI Rosadele (I)	Cat. of tourism in Italy '62-'66; F3 '68 Italy; Temporada Argentina B-A '67
FALK Eva Maria (D)	Germany 2003
FAWCET Marjorie (GB)	Le Mans '38 – Morgan
FERRARI (de) (F)	St Raphaël '54
FERRIER Nadège (F)	Tour de Corse '57 – Dauphine; '58 – Porsche 356; '60 – Simca; Tour de France '59 – P356
FILIPPIS de MariaTheresa (I)	Terramo '50; Mille Miles '50 – Urania; Mille Miles '55 – Maserati; GP Monaco '58 – Maserati 250F; GP Porto '58 – Maserati; Spa; Silverstone
FISHER Sarah (USA)	USA Indy 500 2000-2002
FITLER Clarence (USA)	USA Cape May NJ '05
FIZET (F)	St Raphaël '54
FLAMBART (F)	Rallye Yonne '54 – 2CV
FONTAINE Yvette (F)	Trophy Silverstone – 70 Escort; Zolder '72 – Escort; Le Mans '74 – Chevron; '75 – Porsche; Spa '67 – NSU; '72 – Escort TC; '75 – BMX 3.0 CSL
FONTANA Angela	Tour de Corse '56 – Siata Zagato; '62
FOREST (des) Simone (F)	St Raphaël '31, '32 – Rosengart; Monte Carlo '34 – Peugeot 301; Monte Carlo '35 – Triumph; Monte Carlo '36 – Delahaye; Liège-Rome-Liège '50 – Peugeot; Monte Carlo '53 – Porsche 356; Mille Miles '53 – 4CV
FOSTER Martha (USA)	USA '04-'08
FRAICHNEY Pat (GB)	GB '56
FRANCOIS-SIGRAND Ginette (F)	Monte Carlo '51 203
FREEMAN Joey (GB)	Goodwood '58 – Morris 1000; Brands Hatch '60 – Sprite

FREGONI (F)	St Raphaël '54
FRIEDRICH Renée (F)	Monte Carlo '31 – Bugatti; St Raphaël '32 – Delage
FRISCH Edith (CH)	Germany '30 – Opel; Alpenfahrt '34
GADOU (F)	Tour de France '80 – R5 Alpine
GALICA Divina (ex-ski champion) (GB)	Oulton Park '74 – Escort, Formule 5000 '76 Surtees; F1 Brands Hatch '76; Sports 2000 '77 – Lola; HesKeth F1 '78
GALLIFORD Rona (GB)	Brands Hatch '61 – Mini; Nürburgring '62 – BMW
GARDNER Debra (USA)	USA '84
GAST (du) Camille (Camille Desinge) (F)	Paris-Berlin '01 – Panhard; Paris-Madrid '03 – De Dietrich
GEOFFRE (F)	Monte Carlo '35 – Citroën
GERARD Annie (F)	St Raphaël '60s
GERARD Joan (GB)	Shelsley-Walsh '48 – ERAR6B; Brighton Road Race '47 – Riley Sprite; Silverstone '48; Brighton '48 – ERA
GEURIE Pascale (F)	Le Mans '78 – Lola T298
GIBBS Bluebelle (GB)	Norton side-car '30, HRG 48, Cooper-Climax, Lola 61
GILKA-BOTZOV Bea (D)	Germany '30
GILLIER (F)	Tour de France '75 – BMW 30 CSI
GIRARD (F)	Tour de France '73 – 911S
GNUDI Paola (I)	MM '47 – Fiat 500
GODDBAN (GB)	Coastwald Hill '34 – Singer
GOLDSMITH Gillian (Fortescue-Thomas) (GB)	Shelsley-Walsh '81 – Anson V8, Lotus 23B; Escort Trophy '71 – Mini, TVR, Spa '72, '73 – Escort; '89 – Aston DB4; Shelsley-Walsh '99 – HWM
GOODWIN Nathalie (GB)	GB '68
GORDINE Régine (F)	Monte Carlo '50 – Simca 8; Monte Carlo '51 – Simca 8 Sport; Le Mans '50; Liège-Rome-Liège '50-'54 – Simca, 203; Tour de France '52 – 4CV; Coupe des Alpes '54 – 203
GORDON-SIMPSON E (GB)	Monte Carlo '32 – Singer; Brooklands '35 – Vale
GOUGH (GB)	Shelsley-Walsh '30 – MG; Monte Carlo '33 – Riley
GRANDRIVE (de la) Martine (de Cortanze) (F)	Team Monte Carlo-Beaumont
GRANDVUINET (F)	Tour de France '84 – Visa Chrono
GREGG Deborah (USA)	USA '83
GREGOIRE Renée (F)	Monte Carlo '54 – 203; St Raphaël '54 – 203
GRIOLET (F)	Tour de France '33 – Peugeot
GRIPPER AG (GB)	Brooklands '32 – Frazer-Nash
GRIVA	Rallye Amazon '66 – DS19
GROSVENOR Lady Mary (GB)	Grandsden Lodge '46 – Riley; Bugatti, Frazer-Nash; Shelsley-Walsh '50 – Alta
GROUNDS L (GB)	Monte Carlo '53 – Austin A40; Rallye Tulipes '55 – TR2
GROVE J A (GB)	Monte Carlo '31 – Austin
GUICHARD (F)	Tour de France '77 – VW Golf
GUTHRIE Janet (USA)	Indy 500 '68, '78
HAERLIN Frieda (D)	Germany '30
HAIG Betty (GB)	Marseilles '36 – Singer; St Raphaël '37 – MG; Alpine Trial '46 – AC; '49 – MG; Monte Carlo '50 – MG; Monte Carlo '55 – Standard; '58 – TR3; Le Mans '51 – Ferrari 166 MM; GP Porto '50 – Ferrari; Silverstone '53 – MG
HALL Anne (Mlle Newton) (GB)	RAC '51, '52 – XK120; '55 – Sunbeam Talbot; Tulipes '54; Monte Carlo '55; Monte Carlo '59; RAC '59, '60 – Zéphir; '60-'62 – Anglia; Tulip '62 – TVR; '64 – Falcon; Liège-Rome-Liège '55-'64 – Ford
HALL E. R. (GB)	Shelsley-Walsh '30 – Bentley
HAMMERSLEY Alexandra and Geneviève (F)	Monte Carlo '51, '53 – 203; Tour de France '51; Liège-Rome-Liège '51-'53 – 203; St Raphaël '53
HAMPSON Daisy (GB)	GB '08
HANDLEY-PAGE Mary (GB)	Rallye Tulipes '56 – Std 8; Monte Carlo '58 – Zéphyr
HARKER (GB)	Monte Carlo '34 – Sunbeam
HARMAN (GB)	Monte Carlo '49 – Alvis
HARRIS Dorothy (GB)	Monte Carlo '58 – MGA
HASKEL Isabelle (Mme Alejandro de Tomaso) (I)	USA and Italy '55
HAWKES Gwenda (voir Stewart) (GB)	-
HEDGE G (GB)	Brooklands '32 – Talbot 90
HEIDENDAHL	Monte Carlo '62 – Daf
HENN Bonnie (USA)	-
HENN Margot (D)	Champion German Rallye '82 – Fiesta; Monte Carlo '83 – Alfasud TI

HENNERICI Mercedes	90H Nürburgring '71 – BMW 2002
HENRIO (F)	St Raphaël '51 – Cadillac
HERVE (F)	Tour de France '33 – Peugeot
HERVEUX Jeanne (F)	Côte de Gaillon, du Mont Ventoux – Werner 4cyl; Deauville, Château-Thierry, '09, '10 et avion Blériot
HEUZE Nicole (F)	Tour de France '63
HILLIER Ruth	Monte Carlo '83 – Alfasud TI
HOBS Sunny (USA)	-
HOEPFNER Marianne (Trintignant) (F)	St Raphaël '69-'72 – A110; Tour de France '72 – Alpine; '78 – CX; Tour de Corse '72 – A110; '77 – Célica; '78 –127; Monte Carlo '79 – CX GTI; Le Mans '75-'78 – Stratos and Moynet, WM; Maroc '75, '76; Bandama '73; London-Sidney '77 – Fiat 131; Himalaya '81 – Célica
HOHENLOHE Princess	Course de côte du Kausen '24, '25 – Bugatti
HOLSTE	Monte Carlo '28 – Adler
HONORE Marie (F)	Course de Côte de Crand'Escale '54 – Alfa TI; Tour de France '54 – Alfa; St Raphaël '55 – Alfa TI; Rallye Alpes '56 – Alfa; Lyon-Charbo '58 – Giulietta
HOOKE Jane (GB)	Mallory Park – Lotus Elite
HOUNSFIELD	St Raphaël '54
HOWELL (Mrs John) (USA)	USA 1899 first female driver's license in USA
HOWELL Kathleen (GB)	GP Australie '31 – Riley; Monte Carlo '32 – Riley 9
HURE	St Raphaël '51 – Cadillac
HURTGEN Claudia	F3 Monaco '93, Nürburgring, Singen, FIAGT2 '97 – Porsche; Macau 2000 – Ford Focus; Daytona 2001 – Porsche 911 GT3R; Sebring 2001 – Lola-Nissan
HUSTINX Fernande (Mme de Cortanze) (F)	Tour de France '31 – Mathis; Tour de France '33 – Peugeot; Monte Carlo '33-'35 – Peugeot 301; Tour de France '36 – Hotchkiss; Monte Carlo '52 – 203; Liège-Rome-Liège '50-'52 – 203
ICKX Vanina (B)	Spa '99 – Renault Mégane; Modena Challenge 2000 – Modena 360; Spa – Peugeot 306; Paris-Dakar 2000 – Toyota; Le Mans 2001 – Viper
IMBERT Eliane (F)	Monte Carlo '53 – 356; St Raphaël '54
ITIER Anne-Cécile (F)	Paris-Pau '26 – Brasier; Monte Carlo '39; Hannomag '51 – 4CV; Le Mans 34 – MG; '35 – Fiat; '37 – Adler; '38 – MG; '39 – Simca; Monte Carlo '48-'53 – 4CV
JARDINE (F)	Monte Carlo '31 – Lancia
JEANNE (F)	Tour de France '30 – Rosengart; Monte Carlo '31 – Rosengart
JENKINS Katie (USA)	USA '50
JENNKY Janine (F)	Course côte Gometz-Le-Châtel '28; GP Dijon – Bugatti; Côte de Gaillon – Bugatti; GP Spain '28
JOHANY (F)	Tour de France '70 – Capri
JOHNS (GB)	Monte Carlo '56 – Austin A90
JOHNSON Amy (GB)	St Raphaël '38 – Talbot Lago; Shelsley-Walsh '38 – BMW 328; RAC – Bentley; Monte Carlo '39 – Ford
JOHNSTON	-
JONES (GB)	Liège-Rome-Liège '58 – Austin-Healey
JONES Hermine (USA)	USA 1909 – Maxwell
JOURDAN (F)	Tour de France '33 – Citroën; '35, '36 – Licorne
JULIEN Dominique (Mme Claude Laurent) (F)	-
JUMEAUX-LAFOND (F)	St Raphaël '54
JUNEK Elisabeth (Cz)	TargaFlorio '27, '28 – Bugatti
JUNKERS	Monte Carlo '36, '37 – Plymouth
KASATSKY	Monte Carlo '30 – Chrysler
KASSE Michèle (F)	'50
KEVELOS Olga (GB)	Brandshatch '50, '51 – Kieft 500cc, F3
KING Anita (USA)	USA, '15
KIRK Jo	-
KLEINSCHMIDT Jutta (D)	Paris-Dakar '88; Pharaon '87; Paris-CapeTown '92; Pharaon '92; Dubai '93; Dakar '99; 2000/2001 – Mitsubishi
KLINGER-OOST Minki	Autriche '30, '31 – Maserati
KOENIG Gabrielle (GB)	GB '69
KONDRATIEFF Judy (Mlle Wood) (USA)	California '60 – Mini; Sebring; Riverside GP '71 – BRM
KOPPENHAGUE Corinne (F)	Champion French National Women's Criterium '70 – Porsche; Tour de France '70, '71 – 911S '74 –Alfa GTV6; Rallye Antibes – 104 ZS; Le Mans '76 – Toj; Paris-Dakar '83-'88
KOTTULINSKY Suzanne	RAC '80 – Ascona; RAC '84 – Volvo; Swedish Rallye '84; German Champion '87 – Quattro; Ibiza Cup '89; Swedish Champion '90-'95
KOZMIAN Maria Ludwika (CH)	'20, '30 – Klausen; GP de Berne
KRAMER Louise (Miss Firebird) (USA)	Dixie 500 Atlanta '68

KRAUSE	Monte Carlo '30 – DKW
KRONBAUEROVA	St Raphaël '39 – Jawa
LABBE (F)	Rallye Jeanne d'Arc '54 – Simca
LABOUCHERE (F)	Monte Carlo '34 – Singer; Liège-Rome-Liège '33, '34 – Singer
LABROUSSE (F)	Paris-Spa 1899
LACE	Monte Carlo '38, '39 – Talbot-Darracq
LAFARGUE de GRANGENEUVE (F)	Monte Carlo '52 – Vedette
LAMBERJACK Louise (F)	Monte Carlo '35 – Ford; '36 – Hotchkiss; '39 – Matford
LANG (F)	Tour de France '30, '31 – Rosengart
LANGLOIS (F)	St Raphaël '59 – Dauphine Gord
LARGEOT Suzanne (F)	Le Mans '37-'39 – Simca; Monte Carlo '38 – Matford; Monte Carlo '39 – Hotchkiss
LARKINS (GB)	Shelsley-Walsh '05 – Wolseley
LASHWOOD (GB)	Monte Carlo '53 – Allard
LAUMAILLE (F)	Marseille-Nice 1898
LAURENT Marie (F)	Challenge Simca '70 – CG; Tour de France '72 – BMW 2002 TI; Le Mans '74 – Chevron B23
Le BIGOT (F)	Tour de France '30 – Rosengart
LEAVENS Joyce (GB)	Monte Carlo '54 – Jowett-Javelin
LEBLANC (F)	Tour de France '29 – Peugeot; Tour de France '30-'32 – La Licorne; St Raphaël '33 – Peugeot; Monte Carlo '33-'36 – Peugeot; Liège-Rome-Liège '35 – Peugeot
LEVITT Dorothy (GB)	Speed Trial '03 – Gladiator; Hereford Mille Miles Trial '04 – De Dion; Shelsley-Walsh '05 – Napier; Côte Gaillon '07 – Napier
L'HUILLIER (F)	Tour de France '84 – Visa
LIETARD Mme (F)	St Raphaël '29, '30, '32 – Salmson
LINDH	Monte Carlo '32 – Hudson
LINZ (Mrs FJ) (USA)	USA '08 – founded the first automobile club
LISTER Henrietta (GB)	Brooklands '28 – Aston-Martin
LOCKE-KING Ethel (GB)	Brooklands '07 – Itala 40HP
LOIZY (de) (F)	Monte Carlo '54 – 4CV
LOMBARDI Lella (I)	Le Mans '75 – Alpine; '76 – Stratos; '77 – Inaltera; '78 – Osella; F1 British GP – Brabham; GP Spain
LONGHI-GORLA Olga (I)	Mille Miles '37 – Fiat 508
LOWE Marion (USA)	USA '54
LUZEAUX	Liège-Rome-Liège '34 – Salmson
MAAS Elfreida (USA)	USA '08 and '34
MACONOCHIE	Brooklands '28 – Salmson, Amilcar
MANDELLI Antonella (I)	Tour de Corse '78 – Fiat 127; '83
MANVILLE (GB)	GB '08
MARENGI Erica (I)	Tour de Corse '77 – Fiat 127
MAREUSE Marguerite (F)	Monte Carlo '33, '34, '36 – Peugeot 301; Le Mans '30, '31, '33 – Bugatti
MARIKA (Mme Ragazzi)	Monte Carlo '26 – Citroën B12
MARINOVITCH (F)	Monte Carlo '35-'38 – Matford; Liège-Rome-Liège '35 – Delahaye
MARSHALL	Monte Carlo '50 – MG
MARTELLI-GERI Irma (I)	MM '47 – Fiat
MARTIN (GB)	Brooklands '27, '28 – Riley 9; Monte Carlo '33 – Hilmann; St Raphaël '54
MASON Cynthia (GB)	Mille Miles RAC rallye '35 – Singer
MATHIEW (F)	Tour de Corse '64 – Ti super
MAYMAN Pauline (GB)	Acropole '62 – Healey; RAC '62 – Healey; Coupe des Alpes '63 – Mini; Monte Carlo '63, '64 – Mini; Liège-Rome-Liège '64 – MGB; Tour de France '64, '65 – Cooper S
McCLUGGAGE Denise (USA)	Thompson '56 – XK140; Nassau '56 – Porsche 550; Venezuela '57 – Porsche; Sebring '58 – Fiat Abarth; '59 – Osca 187S; Tour Auto '63 – Mini; Liège-Rome-Liège '63 – Cortina; '64 – Falcon
McDONNEL Pat	South Africa '38
McKENZIE Margaret (GB)	GB '63
McUSTRICH P	Brooklands '34 – Talbot
MEESON (GB)	Brooklands '28
MEINECKE	Monte Carlo '56 – Fiat 1100
MELCHER (GB)	Brooklands '28

MELIN	Monte Carlo '36 – Ford
MELISS (GB)	GB '30
MERCK Ernes (D)	Germany. Klausen '27
MERCREDY Mrs (GB)	Glendhew Hillclimb '03; '04 – DeDion
MERLE (GB)	Tour de Corse '57 – Dauphine
MERMOD Marie- (F)	Coupe Salon '64 – MkII Jag
MEUNIER (GB)	Liège-Rome-Liège '57 – DB; Tour de Corse '57, '58 – DB; Tour de France '58 – DB
MICKEL Agnes (GB)	Shelsley-Walsh '63 – Cooper Climax; '67 – McLaren M3A
MILANI Anna-Maria (I)	St Raphaël '54
MILLER Marilyn (USA)	USA '57
MILLER A G (GB)	Brooklands '29 – Benz 2.5 l
MILLER Nancy (GB)	Shelsley-Walsh '54 – Cooper-Jap
MIMS Dona Mae (USA)	USA '59-'63
MINIER (F)	Tour de France '72 – BMW 2002 TI
MITCHELL Nancy (GB)	Eastbourn Rallye '47 – HRG; Aplies '49; St Raphaël '51; RAC '51; Monte Carlo '53 – Daimler; Prescott '53 – 1100 Cooper; Monte Carlo '53 – Alvis; '54 – Zéphir; '55, '56 – MG; Liège-Rome-Liège '54-'58 – Ford, MG, Healey; Alpes '60 – Mini
MOBLEY Ethel (USA)	USA '49
MOLANDER-BARTH Greta (S)	Monte Carlo '34 – Chysler; '35-'38 – Dodge; '39 DKW; '49 – Dodge; '50-'52 Saab; '54 – Aronde; '55 – DKW; '56 – Mercedes; '58-'62, '73 – Saab
MONDOLINI (F)	Tour de Corse '61-'63 – Dauphine
MONTGOLFIER (de) Cécile (F)	École Paul-Ricard '70 – Berlinette Alpine
MORARIU Hélène	Coupe des Alpes '12, '13 – Puch
MOREAU (F)	Tour de France '54 – 4CV 1063
MOREL (F)	Tour de Corse '57 – Denzel
MOREL Yvonne (GB)	Crystal Palace '38 – MG; Le Mans '37 – MG; Brooklands '38
MORLEY Valerie (Mlle Domleo) (GB)	RAC '57, '58 – Morgan; RAC '59 – TR3; Monte Carlo '61; Alpine Rallye '64; Monte Carlo '67; BMC
MORRIS Violette (F)	Tour de France '23 – Benjamin; Bol d'Or '22, '23, '26, '27 – Benjamin; Bol d'Or '28 – BNC; Paris-Pyrénées '22, '23; Paris-Nice '23, '27; GP San Sebastian '26; Dolomites '34
MOSS Pat (Mrs Carlsson) (GB)	RAC '62 – A-Healey; Rallye Genève '62 – Mini Cooper; Liège-Rome-Liège '57-'64 – Morris, Healey, Cortina, Saab, Sprite; Tour de Corse '60-'68 – Healey, Lancia HF, Alpine A110; Monte Carlo '59-'72 etc.
MOUTON Michèle (F)	Tour de Corse '74-'76 – Alpine, '77-'80 – Fiat 131; '81-'85 – Audi Quattro; Monte Carlo '76 – A310; '77-'80 – Fiat 131; Rallye Champion '81-'85 – Audi Quattro; '86 – 205 T16; Le Mans '75 – Moynet LM; Pikes Peak 8485 – Audi Quattro.
MUELENAERE (de)	Monte Carlo '32 – Talbot
MULL Evelynn (USA)	USA '55
MULLER Cathy (F)	Karting '79; Volant Elf '81 – R5; Albi F3 '84; F3000 season '86; F3 season '87; 905 Spider Cup '95
MULLER-LEUFKENS (D)	Monte Carlo '39 – Hansa
MUNARETTO Erica (I)	'97
MUNTER Leilani (USA)	Nascar 2002
MUNZ Emma (CH)	Switzerland '29
MURISON (GB)	GB '03
MURPHY Paula (USA)	USA '58; '70
NAISMITH Eirane (Paddy) (GB)	Brooklands '32 – Salmson
NATACHA (F)	Tour de France '74, '76, '77 – Alpine
NEEDHAM	Monte Carlo '54 – Ford Consul; Liège-Rome-Liège '54 – Ford
NEIL A and C (GB)	Monte Carlo '54-'56 – Standard Vanguard; 58
NEUMAN (von) Josie	'93
NEWCASTEL (Duchesse de) (GB)	Monte Carlo '54 – Sunbeam T90
NEWTON Mary (GB)	GB '50 – XK120 (sister of Anne Hall)
NEYRET (F)	Tour de France '84, '86 – Visa Chrono
NICE Hellé (Hélène Delangle) (F)	Record Montlhéry '29 – Bugatti; GP Morocco '30; Le Mans '30; Courses demo USA '30; Reims, Dieppe, Comminges, Monza '31; GP Nimes, Dieppe, Marseille '32; St Raphaël '32; Klausen, Ventoux '32; GP Grenoble '31; La Baule '31; GP Marseille '33 – Bugatti; Coupe des Alpes '33 – Bugatti 43; GP Monza '33 – Alfa 8C; St Raphaël '34 – Alfa Monza 8C; Nürburgring '34; Dieppe, Comminges, GP Alger '34; GP Comminges '35; GP Pau '35; Montjuic '35 – Alfa Monza; Monte Carlo '36 – Matford; Tour de France '36 – Matford; GP Pau-LaTurbie; GP Rio de Janeiro, Sao Polo '36 – Rec Yacco; Montlhéry '37 – Matford; Rallye Chamonix '36 – DKW; Péronne, Comminges '39 – Juva4; Monte Carlo '49 – 4CV; GP Nice '51 – 4CV
NIONCEL (F)	St Raphaël '59 – Dauphine Gord

NODES Beate (D)	Germany '84
NORLING	Monte Carlo '49 – Buick; Monte Carlo '51 – Hotchkiss; Monte Carlo '53 – Simca 8
NORTHCOT (GB)	Brooklands '25 – BAC 1,3 l
NYSTROM Liz	GB '64
OKSALA (S)	Tour de Corse '77 – Celica
ORSINI Comtesse Victoria (I)	Monte Carlo '36 – Salmson
OSBORN D	Monte Carlo '56 – Standard-Vanguard; Rallye Tulipes '56 – Std.
OSTERBERG Sylvia	Monte Carlo '63, '64 – Volvo 122; '67 – R8G; Tour de Corse '67 – R8G; Monte Carlo '67 – R8G
OUKI	Tour de Corse '76 – 104 ZS
OZANNE Pat ('Tish') (GB)	Rallye Tulipes '58, '59; Genève '60 – Mini; Monte Carlo '58 – TR3; '62 – Mini Cooper; team A Soisbault '60-'64 – Cortina GT; Sherry Rallye '70 – Austin Maxi; Donegal '73 – Cooper S
PABST Linda (USA)	USA '94
PACE Ada 'Sayonara' (I)	Tour de Corse '59 – Alfa; GP Cuba '60 – Osca MT4
PAGAN Maria 'Mopsy' (USA)	USA '54
PAGET Dorothy (Miss Windham) (GB)	Shelsley-Walsh '30 – Mercedes; Brooklands '31 – Bentley, Mercedes
PAGO Marguerite (I)	Italy '56
PAINDAVOINE (F)	St Raphaël – Bugatti
PALAYER Marie-Pierre (F)	Tour de France '70 – 911S; Tour de France '71 – Alpine; St Raphaël '70; Bandama '73 – 504i
PARNELL (GB)	Monte Carlo '36 – Hilmann
PARSONS Goldie (USA)	USA '65
PATTEN	Monte Carlo '35 – Alvis; '36 Salmson
PATTERSON Louise (USA)	USA '11
PEDELAHORE (F)	Tour de France '71 – Datsun 1600 S
PEDUZZI Anna (La Marocchina) (I)	Mille Miles '33 – Alfa 6C; '53 – Stanguellini; Come-Lieto-Colle '52 – Alfa 1900; Targa Florio '54; Mille Miles '54 – Stanguellini 750
PERRIER Colette (F)	St Raphaël '60s
PERRIER Dominique (F)	Monte Carlo '83 – Alfasud TI; Trophée Visa '82
PETIT Christiane (F)	Tour de Corse '61 – Alfa Giulietta; Tour de France '63 – Porsche 356; '66, '67 – R8G; Tour de France '63 – 356; Tour de Corse '62, '63 – 356; Charbo '67 – R8G
PETRE Kay (GB)	Shelsley-Walsh '35-'37 – Riley; Brooklands '31 – Wolseley Daytona; Brooklands '33, '35 – Bugatti; '34, '35 – Delage V12; Le Mans '34, '35 – Riley; Brooklands '36 – ERA; Safrica GP '37 – Riley and GP Auto Union; Le Mans '37 – Austin; Alpine Rallye and Monte Carlo '39
PEUVERGNE Annick (F)	Tour de Corse '75 – A110
PIAZZA Bianca Maria (I)	Italy '54
PIC (F)	Rallye Sables-d'Olonnes '54
PINK Winifred (GB)	Shelsley-Walsh '23 – Aston Martin
PIRIE Valerie (F)	'64
PITT Cathy (F)	St Raphaël – R8G
PITTONI Franca (I)	Mille Miles '50 – Fiat Topolino
PIZOT (F)	St Raphaël '59 – DB
PLACQ Marie-Françoise (F)	Monte Carlo '83 – Alfasud TI
POCHON Madeleine (F)	Tour de France '51 – 203; '52 – 4CV 1063; '54 – Alfa TI; Monte Carlo '52 – Aronde; '53 – 4CV; '54 – 4CV; '55 – Alfa 1900 TI; Rallye Aixen P '54 – 4CV; Rallye Dauphine '54 – Alfa
POINTET Lucette (F)	St Raphaël '59 – DB Panhard; Tour de Corse '62, '70 – DS21; Monte Carlo '62 – Volvo; '65-'67 – ID 19; East African Safari '65 – DS19; Londres-Sidney '68 – Cortina Lotus
POLENSKY Ingeborg	Team G Thirion
PONS Fabrizia (I)	'76 – A112 Gr1, Kadet GTE; '77, '78 Champion Italy; World Rallye Champion '81 with Michèle Mouton – Audi; Pikes Peak '83; Chine '97; San Remo '98
POWELL Nettie (USA)	USA '09 – Maxwell
POZZOLI (F)	Tour de Corse '56 – Dyna Panhard
PREVOST (F)	St Raphaël '54
PROD'HOMME (F)	Tour de France '84 – 205 GTI
QUERHERNO (F)	Tour de France '84 – Visa
RACLE (F)	Tour de Corse '61 – DKW
RADISSE Lucienne (F)	St Raphaël '31 – Prima4 Renault; Paris-Nice – Delage D8
RAMPINELLI	Monte Carlo '54 – Opel
RAMSEY Alice (USA)	President of the Auto Club America

RANSOM Sue (AUS)	Australia '84
REECE B. G. (GB)	Shelsley-Walsh '33 – Frazer Nash
RENAUD Lise (F)	Tour de Corse '65 – R8G; Mille Miles '57 – DS19
RENAULT Gabrielle (F)	Monte Carlo '66 – R8; Tour de Corse '57 – Aronde; '61 – Dauphine
RENIER Martine (F)	Tour de France '71 – A110; '72, '73 – Alfa; Le Mans '74, '76 – Porsche
RENSHAW Deborah (USA)	USA 'ARCA'
REZZONICO Luisa (I)	St Raphaël '54 – Lancia Aurelia
RICHARDSON	Monte Carlo '33 – Ford
RICHERT Loretta	Hawai '50
RICHIER-DELAVAU (F)	Monte Carlo '36 – Delage
RICHMOND Joan (GB)	Brooklands '32 – Riley 9; GP Ballot 3l; Monte Carlo '32 – Riley; '36 – Triumph; Le Mans '35 – MG; '37 – Ford; Shelsley-Walsh '37 – Fuzzi
RICKEY (USA)	USA '08
RIDELL-MOY Joan (GB)	Monte Carlo '34 – AC; St Raphaël '36 – MG; Le Mans '37 – MG
ROBERTSON	GP Australia '31 – Riley; Brooklands; Monte Carlo '32 – Riley
ROBINSON Shawna (USA)	USA 'ARCA'
ROEHRS Lilian (D)	Germany '30
ROGIER (F)	Liège-Rome-Liège '37 – Delahaye
ROMET (F)	St Raphaël '54
ROOSDORP Anni	Grenzhandring '49 – Veritas
ROPER Lilian (GB)	Shelsley-Walsh '23 – AC
ROSATI Gina (USA)	USA '80
ROSQVIST Ewie (baronne von Korf) (S)	Monte Carlo '60 – Volvo 544; '61 – Volvo 122; '62 – 544; '63, '64 – Mercedes; Liège-Rome-Liège '62, '63 – Mercedes; Argentina GP '62-'65
ROSSETTI Maddy	St Raphaël '54 – Simca Aronde
ROUAULT Germaine (F)	Monte Carlo '33-'39 – Renault, Salmson, Matford; '50-'56 – Simca 8, Aronde, 4CV; St Raphaël '35, '36, '38 – Delahaye; 3H Marseille '36, '37 – Delahaye 135; Le Mans '38 – Amilcar; Le Mans '50 – Simca-Gordini; Liège-Rome-Liège '34 – Salmson; Spa '49 – Talbot; '50 – Simca; Jeanne-d'Arc '54 – 4CV
ROUFF Christine (F)	Tour de France '72 – Alpine
ROURE Nicole (F)	St Raphaël '60s
ROUX Claude (F)	St Raphaël '54 – 203
ROUX Fernande (Mme Mestivier) (F)	GP Reims '36 – Amilcar Pégase; St Raphaël '37-'39 – Amilcar Pégase; Le Mans '38 – Amilcar; Tour de Corse '59 – Dauphine
ROWAN-HAMILTON	Monte Carlo '39 – Talbot
SAINT JAMES Lynn (USA)	Indy 500; Le Mans '89, '91; Daytona '87, '91; Sebring '91
SAJOUS (F)	Tour de France '31 – Mathis
SAVELKOUL	Monte Carlo '38 – Fiat
SCHELL Lucy (USA)	Monte Carlo '29, '30 – Talbot; Monte Carlo '35, '36 – Delahaye; Tour de France '33 – Talbot 3l; Le Mans '37 – Delahaye; St Raphaël '32 – Bugatti
SCHIR	St Raphaël '54
SCHOU-NILSEN	Monte Carlo '62-'64 – Skoda
SCHWELDER Irène C. (GB)	Brooklands '30 – Alvis; Brooklands '32 – Alvis, Talbot
SCOTT Fifi (USA)	USA '55
SCOTT Jill (GB)	Brooklands '28 – Amilcar, Sunbeam GP
SCOTT Linda (USA)	USA '58
SCOTT-MONCRIEFF Averil (GB)	Bo'ness Hill '50 – Bugatti '37, Bentley, Benz
SEDDIGH Laleh (Iran)	Champion Iran Rallye 2004, 2005; Bahrein 2006 – BMW
SEDGWICK Cynthia (GB)	Shelsley-Walsh '33 – Frazer Nash
SEELIGER Marie	Monte Carlo '29 – Mercedes Benz 2l
SEERS Rosemary (Mlle Vianello) (GB)	Goodwood and Brands Hatch '52-'60 – MG, Cooper, Zephyr, Sprite, Sunbeam Alpine; Liège-Rome-Liège '61 – MG Midget; Rallye Tulipes '61 – Herald; Tour de France '63 – Sunbeam Rapier; Monte Carlo '63 – Falcon
SEGRESTAIN (F)	Rallye Jeanne-d'Arc '54 – Peugeot
SEIGNARD (F)	Tour de France '51 – 4CV
SEIGNOBEAUX (F)	Tour de France '84, '85 – Visa
SELSDON Lady Anne (GB)	500 miles Race 334 – Frazer-Nash
SHAW Georgie (Miss Sterret) (GB)	Mini '69; Escort Ladies' Race – TR7; '76
SHERER M C (GB)	Mille Miles Rallye '36 – MG
SHUTES Betty (USA)	USA '55

SIGRAND Françoise (F)	Monte Carlo '53 – Jowett-Javelin; '54 – 203; '55 – Aronde; Liège-Rome-Liège '53 – 203
SIKO Odette (F)	Montlhéry Record Yacco '37; Monte Carlo '36; Le Mans '30, '31 – Bugatti; '32 – Alfa 6C; '33; Liège-Rome-Liège '34 – Salmson; '35 – Delahaye
SIMON Yvonne (F)	Liège-Rome-Liège '38/'39 – Hotchkiss; Monte Carlo '38/'39; Spa '49 – Talbot; GP Porto '50 – Ferrari 166; Le Mans '50, '51 – Ferrari; Monte Carlo '51 – Simca 8 Sport; St Raphaël '53, '54; Monte Carlo '54 – Aronde
SIMPSON (Mrs Gordon) (GB)	GB '35
SIMS Virginia (USA)	USA '55
SKELTON Betty (USA)	USA '56 – Corvette, Nascar, land speed record
SKINNER Barbara (Carbu. SU, Skinner Union, Mrs John Bolster) (GB)	Shelsley-Walsh '34-'37 – Morris Minor; Le Mans '35 – MG
SLATTER	Monte Carlo '54 – Sunbeam-Talbot
SLAUGHTER Juliette (Mlle Scott-Gun, Mrs J. Brindley) (GB)	Le Mans '78 – Lola T294
SMITH Louise	Nascar, Daytona '46, '47
SMITH Pat (GB)	Rallye Keswick '57 – Austin A35; Rallye Portugal '59 – Mini; London Rallye '61 – Mini; RAC '61; Monte Carlo '61 – Mini; Monte Carlo '62 – Rapier; Scottish '66, '69 – Imp; London-Mexico '70 – Austin 1800; RAC '72 – Capri
SMITH Rosemary Joy (GB)	Monte Carlo '64 – Sunbeam-Rapier; '65, '67 – Hillman Imp; Sebring '70 – Proto; '71 – Lancia HF
SMITH-HAAS Margies (GB)	Le Mans '84, '85 – Porsche 930 and BMW
SMITH-SEERS (GB)	Tour de France '62, '63 – Sunbeam
SOISBAULT Annie (de Montaigu) (F)	Monte Carlo '56 – Aronde; Mille Miles '57 – Panhard; Coupe USA '57 – TR3; Tour de Corse '57 – TR3; '62 – MkII; '63 – Cooper; Liège-Rome-Liège '58-'60 – Triumph Herald, TR3; St Raphaël '59 – TR3; Monte Carlo '58, '59; RAC '59; Acropole '59; Tulipes '58-'60; Sestrières '59 – TR3; Tour de France '57-'59 – TR3; '60 – Porsche; '61 – Fvega; '62, '63 – MkII; '64 – Ferrari GTO; Rallye La Baule '64 – Jaguar MkII; 1000km Paris '64; Ventoux '69 – Alpine
SOL Nicole (F)	Monte Carlo '83 – Alfasud TI; Spa '68 – Alfa 1750
SPEELIGER	Monte Carlo '30 – Mercedes
SPIERS Annie (GB)	Liège-Rome-Liège '59 – Saab
ST JAMES Lynn (USA)	5000 Miles Indy
STACKELBERG	Monte Carlo '33, '34 – Huppmobile
STANILAND	Monte Carlo '32 – Riley
STANLEY-TURNER Dorothy (GB)	Crystal Palace '38 – MG; Le Mans '37 – MG; Brooklands '38; Shelsley-Walsh Hill '39 – Alta; Brooklands '39 – MG-Q; Monte Carlo '52, '53 – Alvis
STANTON (GB)	Monte Carlo '34 – Riley
STARKEY Laura (GB)	Shelsley-Walsh 1913 – Sunbeam
STEMBERT (F)	Liège-Rome-Liège '55 – Panhard
STEWART Gwenda (Hawkes) (GB)	Montlhéry Record '33 – Derby-Miller; Le Mans '34, '35 – Derby Sport, Derby-Maserati; Brooklands '35 Speed Queen – Derby-Miller
STILLE (F)	Monte Carlo '50 – Simca 8
STRESA Betty (F)	St Raphaël '39 – Simca 8
STUFFEL	St Raphaël '54
SUMMERS (GB)	GB '36
SUTHERLAND (duchesse de) (GB)	(President of the Ladies' Autoclub England, '03)
TARZI	Rallye AGACI '64 – TR4
TAYLOR-MATTHEWS Anita (GB)	Charterhall '63 – Lotus Elan; Silverstone – Anglia; Tour de France '64 – Spitfire; Canadian Shell – Cortina Lotus; British Touring Series '65 – Anglia, Cortina, Mustang 350 GT; Nassau – Mustang; 6H Brands Hatch – MGBGT
TAYLOUR Fay (Irl)	Shelsley-Walsh '33 – MG K3; Brooklands '30-'32 – Talbot 105; '33 – Alfa Monza; Crystal Palace '34; Leinster Trophy; Adler Trumph; Mille Miles – Aston-Martin; Brooklands – Salmson, Bentley, Frazer-Nash; South African GP '38 – Riley; Brooklands '50 – Cooper 500cc
TERRAY Irène (F)	Monte Carlo '53 – 4CV; Monte Carlo '54 – 203 spec; Liège-Rome-Liège '52 – Peugeot; '53-'55
TEXIER Louisette (F)	Tour de France '61 – Alfa TI; '64 – MkII; Monte Carlo '59 – Aronde; '62 – Alfa
THIBAULT (F)	Liège-Rome-Liège '34 – Peugeot; St Raphaël '35 – Peugeot
THIRION Gilberte (B)	Rallye Soleil de Cannes '51, '54 – 356; St Raphaël '52-'54; Rallye Charbo '54, '56; Rallye Tulipes '53; Rallye Morocco '53, '54; Spa '53 – Fiat; Tour de France '53; Eifel Renn '53; 1000km Nürburgring '54; 24H Francorchamps '53; Mille Miles '54 – Gordini; '55, '56; 12H Reims '56; Monte Carlo '56; Tour de France '54 – Porsche 356; Tour de Corse '56 – Dauphine; Monte Carlo '56; 1000km Paris '54; Tour de Corse '54; 12H Sebring '57
THOMAS (F)	Tour de France '33 – Amilcar
THOMAS Jill (GB)	GB '28
THOMPSON Muriel	Brooklands '08 – Austin Pebble
THRUPP	'08
TIBESAR Marie-Rose (CH)	Suisse '62
TARNAUD Corinne (C Koppenhague) (F)	'70

TRAUTMANN Claudine (Bouchet and ex-Vanson) '(F)	Liège-Rome-Liège '62, '63 – DS; London-Mexico '70 – DS21; Tour de Corse '67 – Fulvia HF; Tour de France '71
TROUILLAT (F)	-
URQUHART (F)	St Raphaël '54
UTZ (GB)	Brooklands '25 – Alvis
VALET Michèle	Tour de Corse '69; Monte Carlo '70 – 2002 TI; Coupe des Alpes '71 – Alfa Spider
VAN DAMM Sheila (GB)	RAC '51 – Sunbeam; Monte Carlo '54-'56 – Sunbeam T90; Critérium Alpin '53, '54; Mille Miles '57 – Sunbeam; Tulipes '54
VAN LAWICK (baronne)	Monte Carlo '29 – Horsch
VAN LIMBURG-STIRUM (comtesse)	Monte Carlo '49, '50 Ford
VAN OVERSTRAETEN	Liège-Rome-Liège '51 – Pontiac; '52 – Simca; '53 – Panhard
VAN PUYENBROEK	Monte Carlo '52 – Aurelia
VAN STRIEN	Monte Carlo '39 – Ford; '49 – Ford V8
VAN TUYILL VAN SEROOSKERPEN (baronne)	Liège-Rome-Liège '38 – MG
VANONI Evelyne (F)	Team Asepyogyl
VANSON Claudine (Mlle Bouchet and Mme Trautmann) (F)	Monte Carlo '59, '60 – Aronde; '61 – ID 19; Tour de France '61 – DS19; Liège-Rome-Liège '60 – A-Healey; Tour de Corse '59 – Simca; '60 – DS19; '61 – ID 19
VAUGHAN Morna	Monte Carlo '32, '39 – Triumph
VENIEL	-
VENTURI Jole (I)	Mille Miles '30 – OM
VERNEY Annie-Charlotte (F)	Tour de France '74 – Porsche; '77 – Opel Kadett; Le Mans '74-'83 – Porsche and Rondeau; Monte Carlo '79 – Escort
VERSIGNY Charlotte (F)	Monte Carlo '27 – Fiat; '28 – Talbot; Montlhéry '28 – Bugatti; Bol d'Or; St Raphaël
VIDALI Tamara (USA)	USA '51
VREDENBURCH	Monte Carlo '36, '38, '39 – Ford
WADDY (GB)	Brooklands '31 – Lagonda
WAGNER Renée (Mme Chanal) (F)	Team and co-pilot A Soisbault, Mado Blanchoud, Claudine Trautmann, Vice President FFSA
WALKER M (GB)	Monte Carlo '54 – Sunbeam-Talbot; '55 – Standard
WALLRAF	Tour de Corse '58 – DKW; Routes de Nord '69; TAP '68; Maroc '70 – Triumph, Alfa, Chrysler
WARIN Francine (F)	Tour de France '69 – TR6; '70 – Lancia HF
WARUM (F)	Tour de France '71 – Fiat 124; '72 – Fiat 128
WELLESLEY Lady Jane (GB)	Brands Hatch '75 – Ford Escort
WEMBLYN(GB)	Ranelagh Ladies race 1900
WERNER Hannelore (D)	Monte Carlo '70, '71 – BMW 2002 TI
WHEELER Mary (GB)	Goodwood '59 – TR2, TVR, 73
WHINCOP Monica (GB)	GB '47, '49
WHITAKER Amanda (GB)	Formula Ford '92 – TVR Tuscan 2000
WILBY (GB)	Monte Carlo '36 – Armstrong-Siddeley; '39 – Lea-Francis
WILLIS Isobel (GB)	Hill Sprint '58 – Turner, Sprite; RAC '59; Cooper 500; '62, '63 – Imp, Simca 1000
WILLMANN	St Raphaël '54
WILSON Désirée (SA)	F1 GB GP '80 – Williams
WIRTH Ursula	Rallye '61 – Volvo; Monte Carlo '62 – Mercedes; Monte Carlo '64 – Saab
WISDOM Anne 'Wiz' (daughter of Elsie) (Mme Peter Riley) (GB)	Team of Tommy Wisdom and Pat Moss
WISDOM Elsie 'Bill' (GB)	Shelsley-Walsh '30 – FrazerNash; Brooklands '30 – FrazerNash, Leyland-Thomas 7.2l, Riley 9; Le Mans '32, '33 – Aston; '35 – Riley; '38 – MG; Monte Carlo '35 – Chrysler; Brooklands '34 – MG Magnette and Riley; Tourist Trophy race '36 – Fiat; Mille Miles '37 – MG; Alpine Rallye '33 – MG; '34 – Talbot; '51
WORSLEY Victoria (Mrs King-Farlow) (GB)	Brooklands '28 – MG '34 – Talbot
WRIGHT L. (GB)	Brooklands '30 – MG; Brooklands '31 – Austin Ulster; Brighton Road Race '30-'34
WUNSCH Waltraud (D)	Monte Carlo '81, '82, '83 – Alfasud TI
YOSHIKAWA Tomiko (J)	Le Mans '92-'94 – Spice, Courage, Porsche 962
ZAGORNA	Monte Carlo '30
ZURICK Audrey (USA)	'50 – TR3

Acknowledgements

The author would like to thank:

L'ACF, Philippe Bavouzet, Christine Beckers, Marie-Claude Beaumont, Gilles Blanchet, André Binda, Bernard Brulé, Daniel Cabart, Hervé Chevalier, Françoise Conconi, Bernard Consten, André et Christian de Cortanze, Dominique Dubarry, Sacha Gordine, Philippe Hebert, Colas Henckes (Porsche France), Hubert d'Honincthun, Caroline Knuckey, Corinne Koppenhague, Claudine Latouille, Claude Le Maître, Maurice Louche, Jacques Mertens, Jean-Louis Moncet, Jean-Pierre Morlet (Daimler Chrysler), Christophe Mouchoux, Laurence Mouillefarine, Marc Nicolosi, Bob Neyret, Mike Ostrov, Dominique Pascal, Patrimoine Renault, Marie-Aimée Piérard, Thomas Popper, Jacques Potherat (in memoriam), Jean-Pierre Potier, Estelle et Gérard Prévot, Antoine Raffaelli, Johnny Rives, Jean Sage, Annie Soisbault, Louisette Texier, André Vaucourt, Jean-Paul Ventugol, Erik Verhaest, Bernard Viart, Jeremy Wood.

Bibliography

Violette Morris, la hyène de la Gestap, Raymond Ruffin, Le Cherche Midi, 2004, Paris
The Bugatti Queen, Miranda Seymour, Pocket Book, London, 2004
Fast women, John Bullock, Robson Books, London, 2002
Brooklands, W Body, Tee & Whiten and J Mead, London, 1949
The French sports car revolution, Anthony Blight, GT Foulis, Nr Yeoville, 1996
Archives d'une passion, Antoine Raffaelli, Maeght Éditeur, Paris, 1997
Rallyes, anecdotes & histoires vécues, Françoise Conconi, Jean-Michel Fabre, Michel Morelli, E-T-A-I, 2e édition, 2006
Le Mouvement social, A Buisseret
La femme et l'auto, Chantal Hedal, Dargaud, Paris, 1997
La duchesse d'Uzès, Patrick de Gmeline, Parrin, Paris, 2002
Women in motorsport from 1945, Jamieson, Tuthill, Jaker/BWRDC, 2003
Nine Lives plus, The Hon Mrs Victor Bruce, Pelham Books, London, 1977
Pilote et femme, Marie-Claude Beaumont, Solar, Paris, 1971
Roberta Cowell's Story, R Cowell, William Heineman LTD, London, 1954
Atalanta, S C H Davis, GT Foulis, London
24 Heures du Mans 1923-1992, Christian Moity, Jean-Marc Teissèdre, Alain Bienvenu, Éd. d'Art JP Barthélémy/ACO, Le Mans, 1992
Le Rallye de Monte Carlo au XXe siècle, Maurice Louche, Éd. M Louche, Alleins, 2001
Le Tour de France Automobile 1889-1986, Maurice Louche, Éd. M Louche, Alleins, 1987
Un siècle de grands pilotes Français, Maurice Louche, Éd. M Louche, Alleins, 1995
Fay Taylour queen of speedway, Brian Belton, Panther Publishing, High Wycomb, 2002
Mercedes, R W Schlegelmich, Éd. Place des Victoires, Paris, 2004
Unic passe avant tout, Dominique Dubarry, Jacques Grancher Éd., Paris, 1982
Huschke von Hanstein, the racing baron, Tobias Aichele, Köln, 1999
Les Triumph en compétition, Frédéric Reydellet, Éd. F Reydellet, 2003
American Racing, Tom Burnside, Denise McCluggage, Könemann, Köln, 1996
Time & two seats, J Wimpffen, Motor Sport Research Group, Redmond WA, 1999
Open roads and front engines, J Wimpffen, David Bull Publishing, Phoenix AZ, 2005
Motor racing, the golden age, J Tennant, Cassel Illustrated, London, 2004
Die Geschischte der Rallye Monte Carlo, Bernhard Brägger, Éd, Scriptum, Altdorf CH, 1998
1960 Les années chromes, Jean-Marc Thevenet, Éd. Du May, Paris, 1987
The Shelsley Walsh story, Simon Taylor, Haynes Publishing, Yeovil, 2005
Revue Automobilia
Rétroviseur, Dossier Healey et Mini
Irish Times
La vie de l'Auto, portraits – J-C Potier
www.bwrdc.co.uk (British Women Racing Driver's Club)